ROUTLEDGE LIBRARY EDITIONS: SAUDI ARABIA

Volume 4

SAUDI ARABIA 2000

SAUDI ARABIA 2000
A Strategy for Growth

JEAN PAUL CLERON

LONDON AND NEW YORK

First published in 1978

This edition first published in 2015
by Routledge
2 Park Square, Milton Park, Abingdon, Oxon, OX14 4RN

and by Routledge
711 Third Avenue, New York, NY 10017

Routledge is an imprint of the Taylor & Francis Group, an informa business

© 1978 Jean Paul Cleron

All rights reserved. No part of this book may be reprinted or reproduced or utilised in any form or by any electronic, mechanical, or other means, now known or hereafter invented, including photocopying and recording, or in any information storage or retrieval system, without permission in writing from the publishers.

Trademark notice: Product or corporate names may be trademarks or registered trademarks, and are used only for identification and explanation without intent to infringe.

British Library Cataloguing in Publication Data
A catalogue record for this book is available from the British Library

ISBN: 978-1-138-82515-4 (Set)
ISBN: 978-1-138-84626-5 (Volume 4)
Pb ISBN: 978-1-138-84672-2 (Volume 4)

Publisher's Note
The publisher has gone to great lengths to ensure the quality of this reprint but points out that some imperfections in the original copies may be apparent.

Disclaimer
The publisher has made every effort to trace copyright holders and would welcome correspondence from those they have been unable to trace.

SAUDI ARABIA 2000
A STRATEGY FOR GROWTH

JEAN PAUL CLERON

CROOM HELM LONDON

© 1978 Jean Paul Cleron
Croom Helm Ltd, 2-10 St John's Road, London SW11

ISBN 0-85664-560-5

British Library Cataloguing in Publication Data

Cleron, Jean Paul
    Saudi Arabia 2000.
    1. Saudi Arabia – Economic conditions
    I. Title
    330.9'53'805   HC497.A6
    ISBN 0-85664-560-5

Printed in Great Britain by
REDWOOD BURN LIMITED
Trowbridge & Esher

CONTENTS

Preface	9
Part I: The Anatomy of the Saudi Arabian Economy	
1. Introduction	15
2. The Oil Sector	19
3. The Non-Oil Sector	39
4. The Factors of Production	47
5. The Mechanism of Domestic Inflation	65
6. The National Accounts and the Balance of Payments	70
7. The Structure of the Economic System	83
Part II: The Strategies of Economic Development	
8. The Development Process	105
9. The Management of the Economic Development	127
10. Conclusion	151
Bibliography	153
Appendix I	155
Appendix II	162
Index	167

To my wife Micheline

PREFACE

This book is concerned with the economic aspects of Saudi Arabian development in the next three decades. The research is based upon an elaborate analysis of the structure of the economy and approaches the subject matter from a quantitative perspective. The structure of the economy is logically represented by a dynamic simulation model that includes both the mechanism which generates the economic development and the constraints which retard the development process. The purpose of the model is to assess long-term strategies of development on the basis of assumptions referring to policy decisions, structural changes and behavioural patterns. Such a model is not a forecasting tool. It should be viewed as a planning model which is less concerned with proximate effects or specific aspects of the development process than with the global, long-term consequences of policy decisions as well as structural and behavioural changes.

Long-term planning is indeed of extreme importance to Saudi Arabia. The abrupt increase in both the price of crude oil and resulting revenues to the kingdom has allowed the massive planned expenditures of the Second Five-Year Plan, the rapid growth of the kingdom's international trade and a large accumulation of financial assets. These sudden and drastic changes have however taken place within a mainly traditional economy, unprepared to absorb and to cope with a 430 per cent increase in government revenues. Inflation, bottlenecks and severe shortages have therefore risen sharply. Such negative and undesirable consequences of the well known discrepancy between too much money and too few resources are likely to persist and to increase severely the cost of the development programme if the economic activity is not finely regulated.

In 1975, 82 per cent of the kingdom's gross domestic product resulted from the production of crude oil. The massive financial resources generated by the daily production of seven to nine million barrels of crude oil give Saudi Arabia the unique opportunity to move the economy away from its dependence on oil and to achieve a diversified industrialization programme. There exist, however, serious conflicts. Conflict between the absorptive capacity of the economy and the necessity to achieve development before the generalization of crude oil substitutes; conflict between the level of oil production needed to finance the domestic development and the level of production compatible with both OPEC pricing policy and the requirements of the world oil market; conflict between the accumulation of financial assets and the rate of national and international inflation; conflict between a large demand for expatriate labour and the social limits to foreign presence in the kingdom; conflict between a fast growing demand and the physical constraints limiting supply.

The various problems created by these conflicts can seldom be completely eliminated. Careful planning can, however, determine the policy decisions that will minimize, or at least alleviate, the impact of each problem on economic development. Long-term planning is also useful to evaluate the cost and consequences of the economic decisions constituting the foundation of development strategies. Short-term analyses of long-range development programmes are often misleading and may provide significant underestimations of the actual requirements of the proposed programmes which, if such requirements had been correctly evaluated, might not have been implemented.

Such planning must be based upon a global view of the economic system. The planning tools must clearly show the complex mechanism of direct and indirect interrelations between economic and social variables as well as the deep imbrication of problems. This book deals with such planning tools.

The first part of the book analyzes the structure of the Saudi Arabian economy and gives a detailed description of the simulation model. This part is rather technical and can be overlooked by the reader who is primarily interested in the results of the simulations of the model. These results are presented and commented on in the second part of the book.

This study, which is part of a larger programme of research, is one of the results of the continuing research programme of the College of Industrial Management at the University of Petroleum and Minerals, Dhahran, Saudi Arabia. I would like to thank several persons whose comments, help and assistance have facilitated my work and improved the content of this book. Dean Henry Albers and Mr Ali Al-Yusuf provided very valuable assistance in both the organizational and the academic aspects of the research project. Very valuable aid and comments were also provided by Mr Ahmad Al-Sari, Dean Ali Al-Khalaf and Dr Ronald Scott, all of the University of Petroleum and Minerals. Part of the research was conducted at Development Analysis

Associates, Inc. in Cambridge, Massachusetts. The scientific environment within this organization has been highly profitable, especially as far as the modelling phase of the project is concerned. I would like particularly to thank Professor Seifert, Dr Picardi and Dr Shorb. At last, I would like to thank all the students who have attended 'Petroleum Economics' and 'Economics of Saudi Arabia'. Their questions, comments and remarks have helped me in clarifying my ideas and improving my knowledge.

Dhahran, Saudi Arabia Jean Paul Cleron
April 1977

PART I
THE ANATOMY OF THE SAUDI ARABIAN ECONOMY

1 INTRODUCTION

The Saudi Arabian economy must be viewed from a dual perspective. There is a dominant, highly capital-intensive oil sector and a traditional, labour-intensive non-oil sector. In 1975 for example, mining, oil and gas generated 82 per cent of the gross domestic product and employed 3 per cent of the labour force, the remaining 18 per cent being produced by 97 per cent of the labour force.

Because the most significant long-term aspect of the oil sector is the generation of income flows, the structural analysis of this sector is primarily concerned with the revenues resulting from postulated production and pricing policies. In the non-oil sector, the emphasis is on the process of economic growth through productive capital accumulation and labour acquisition. Also important to the long-term development of the economy are the dynamics of the Saudi population, the changes in the balance of trade and payments and the accumulation of financial assets which are also considered by the model.

The method of analysis is based upon both the identification and the analysis of the feedback loops that control the long-term dynamics of the economy. The assemblage of all relevant feedback loops constitutes the postulated structure of the economy, that is, the dynamic simulation model. This model is a system-dynamics model and the simulation language is DYNAMO. The model is divided into ten substructures that mathematically describe the various parts of the economic system. These substructures are: the production of crude oil, the pricing of crude oil, non-oil production, the accumulation of financial assets, the accumulation of productive capital, the Saudi population, the labour force, the national accounts, the balance of payments and the mechanism of domestic inflation.

Figure 1.1 shows the major interrelations constituting the structure of the economic system. The arrows indicate that a change in a given variable generates induced changes in another or several other variables. For example,

| Crude oil production | ⟶ | Gross domestic product |

indicates that an increase (or a decrease) in the production of crude oil

Figure 1.1: Major Interrelations of the Model

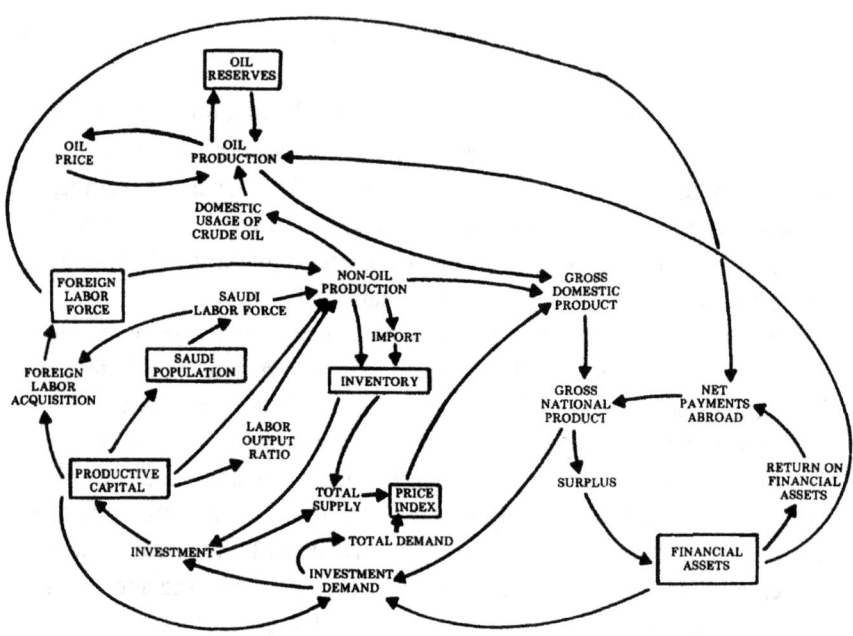

induces, every other variable being kept constant, an increase (or a decrease) in the gross domestic product.

The loops that can be identified in Figure 1.1 are simplified and aggregated. They actually involve more variables and result from the combination of many basic loops that are precisely identified later in this book. Diagrams such as the diagram of Figure 1.1 are useful to an understanding both of the structural links within the economic system and of the mechanisms controlling the various behaviours of the economy.

Each substructure is a model within the model. It is therefore necessary to identify and analyze first the feedback loops of each substructure. Then, the loops that result from the assemblage of the various substructures, such as the loops that are shown in Figure 1.1, can be defined.

The basic elements of a feedback loop are the levels, or the state variables of the model, the flows that control the levels and the auxiliary variables that identify the various elements composing the flows. The physical relationships between level and flows are illustrated in Figure 1.2. Figure 1.3 gives a functional representation of

Introduction

Figure 1.2: Physical Representation of the Relationships between Level and Flows

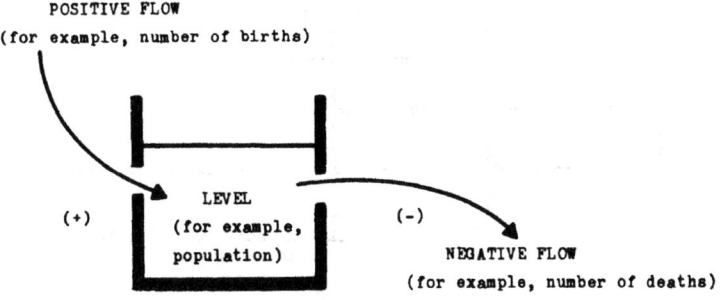

Figure 1.3: Functional Representation of the Relationships between Level, Flows and Auxiliary Variables

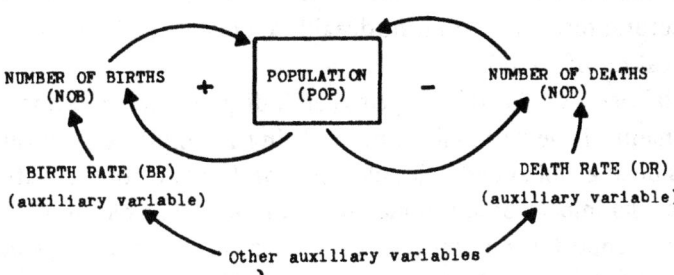

a simple set of relationships between level, flows and auxiliary variables.

The coding of these diagrams in algebraic statements keeps track of the dynamics of the relationships through the system of subscripts shown in Figure 1.4.

Thus, the algebraic formulation of the dynamics of population is

$$POP.K = POP.J + (DT)(NOB.JK - NOD.JK)$$
$$NOB.KL = (BR.K)(POP.K)$$
$$NOD.KL = (DR.K)(POP.K)$$

The model is a set of logical assumptions about the Saudi Arabian economic system composed of twelve levels linked by more than a hundred algebraic relationships. The size of a model depends upon its level of aggregation, i.e. the number of sectors that compose the model,

18 *The Anatomy of the Saudi Arabian Economy*

Figure 1.4: Subscript Conventions of the Model

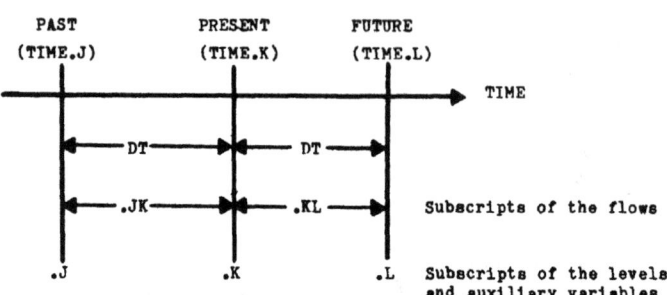

and upon its structural sophistication. Each numerical constant being, in a long-term model, defined for a long period of time, one must make sure that these constants keep a very basic meaning. Thus, constants in a short-term analysis often become variables in a long-term analysis. The transformation of short-term constants into long-term variables is a structural refinement that noticeably increases the level of sophistication of a model.

An elaborate structural analysis is an indispensable operation. The management of the national economy being a complex operation that requires both a global and a detailed approach, i.e. tactics and strategy, the potential impact of any policy decision or social change of reasonable importance upon each element of the economic system must be shown by the structural network of the model. An incomplete structure generates partial analyses usually leading to serious misinterpretations which result from the fact that the aspects of the problem not directly involved are omitted. In the long term, these aspects are usually important and may intensify the severity of the problems the policy decisions were supposed to alleviate. The necessity of an elaborate structural analysis also results from the fact that the overall structure is more important to the behaviour of the system than any of its components. Therefore, the problem of data inaccuracy, especially significant in a long-term analysis, is partly solved by the sophistication of the structure (see Chapter 7).

2 THE OIL SECTOR

Importance of the Sector

The importance of Saudi Arabia's oil sector in terms of both production and revenues is shown in Table 2.1. Saudi Arabia is the first oil-exporting country with respectively 7.4, 8.4 and 6.9 million barrels exported daily in 1973, 1974 and 1975. Saudi Arabia is also the first country in petroleum reserves. From 1938, the first year of production, to 1976, more than twenty-eight billion barrels of crude oil have been produced, that is, twenty-six per cent of the 1975 proven reserves and sixteen per cent of the 1975 probable reserves. This level of production has generated, at the end of 1976, a cumulative revenue of about one hundred billion dollars.

Very significant is the fact that the 1974 income (22.6 billion dollars) is greater than the sum of all previous annual revenues (19.2 billion dollars). As shown in Table 2.2, the contribution of crude oil to the Saudi Arabian gross domestic product is preponderant.

The model regards the oil sector as a generator of income flows and ignores the mechanism of crude-oil production. As a result, both the stock of productive capital allocated to the production of crude oil and the labour force employed in this activity are not taken into consideration. However, the downstream operations such as petroleum refining are included in the non-oil sector. This omission is justified by the fact that the model mainly deals with the economic development of the non-oil sector. Besides, the most important aspect of Saudi Arabia's future economic development is not its ability to produce crude oil, but its ability to transform its natural resources into social and economic development.

The Structure of the Oil Sector

The production of crude oil is an activity that consumes reserves to generate income flows. Therefore, the level of crude oil reserves depends upon the production flows. As production is supposed to be partly dependent upon reserves, the first feedback loop of the oil sector is a negative loop that links production and reserves (Figure 2.2). Saudi Arabia is, however, the only major oil producer in which the growth of proven reserves remains almost constantly higher than the growth in extraction rate (Table 2.3). The first page of the Aramco

Table 2.1: Crude Oil Production, Oil Revenues and Government Budget

	Crude oil production				Oil revenue		Government budget revenues (10^6 SR)
	Daily average (1,000 bbl)	Total (10^6 bbl)	Cumulative (10^6 bbl)	Crude oil price[1] (US \$/bbl)	10^6 US \$	10^6 SR[2]	
1950	546.7	200	719	1.75	56.7	202	n.a.
1951	761.5	278			110.0	390	n.a.
1952	824.8	302			212.2	753	n.a.
1953	844.6	308		1.93	169.8	603	n.a.
1954	961.8	351			236.2	838	n.a.
1955	976.6	356	2,314		340.8	1,210	n.a.
1956	1,002.7	367			290.2	1,029	n.a.
1957	1,030.8	376		2.08	296.3	1,040	1,500
1958	1,058.5	386			297.6	1,058	1,400
1959	1,152.7	421		1.9	313.1	1,111	1,405
1960	1,313.5	481	4,345	1.8	333.7	1,186	2,786
1961	1,480.1	540			377.6	1,342	2,166
1962	1,642.9	600			409.7	1,455	2,452
1963	1,786.0	652			607.7	2,158	2,686
1964	1,896.5	694			523.2	1,857	3,112
1965	2,205.3	805	7,636		662.6	2,354	3,961
1966	2,601.8	950			789.7	2,804	5,025
1967	2,805.0	1,024			909.1	3,227	4,937
1968	3,042.9	1,114			926.8	3,291	5,535
1969	3,216.2	1,174			958.6	3,405	5,966
1970	3,799.1	1,387	13,284		1,213.9	4,310	7,940
1971	4,768.9	1,741	15,024	2.285	1,944.9	6,905	11,120
1972	6,016.3	2,202	17,226	2.479	2,794.5	9,920	15,368
1973	7,596.2	2,773	19,999	2.591–5.036	4,340.0	15,407	22,810
1974	8,479.7	3,095	23,094	11.651–11.251	22,573.5	80,136	98,247
1975	7,075.4	2,583	25,677	12.376	25,676.2	91,151	95,743
1976	8,343.9[3]	3,054	28,731[3]	12.376[4]			

[1] Arabian light. Ras Tanura (34 API)
[2] On the basis of 3.55 riyals for 1 US \$
[3] Aramco only
[4] Situation at 1 November 1976

Sources: OPEC, Saudi Arabian Monetary Agency, Ministry of Finance and National Economy, First National City Bank.

The Oil Sector

Table 2.2: Increase in Gross Domestic Product 1970–1980
(SR millions in constant 1974/75 prices)

	1969/70	1974/75	1979/80
Private			
Agriculture	1,181.0	1,409.0	1,714.3
Crude petroleum and natural gas	52,197.7	121,232.0	195,199.5
Other mining and quarrying	67.7	175.3	352.6
Petroleum refining	6,118.8	7,494.7	9,565.5
Other manufacturing	517.5	901.8	1,736.3
Electricity, gas, water and sanitary services	177.5	333.3	670.4
Construction	1,867.8	4,362.0	8,773.7
Wholesale and retail trade, restaurants and hotels	1,460.8	2,580.0	5,189.4
Transport, communications, and storage	1,801.5	3,637.8	7,317.1
Ownership of dwellings	1,222.9	1,636.7	2,190.2
Finance, insurance, real estate, and other business services	603.0	895.2	1,800.6
Community, social and personal services	345.5	522.4	1,005.8
Less imputed bank service charge	(69.0)	(63.0)	(63.0)
TOTAL Private	67,492.7	145,117.2	235,452.4
Government			
Public administration	920.9	1,291.4	2,079.8
Education	529.7	1,026.8	1,960.0
Health	120.6	256.5	515.9
SUB-TOTAL	1,571.2	2,574.7	4,555.7
Defence	769.3	1,025.4	2,062.5
TOTAL Government	2,340.5	3,600.1	6,618.2
Gross Domestic Product			
(excluding import duties)	69,833.2	148,717.3	242,070.6
Summary (in billions of riyals)			
Crude oil	52.2	121.2	195.2
Petroleum refining	6.2	7.5	9.6
Non-oil	9.2	16.4	30.7
Government sector	2.3	3.6	6.6
TOTAL non-oil	11.5	20.0	37.3
GDP	69.9	148.7	242.1

Source: *Middle East Economic Digest*, 22 August 1975.

22 *The Anatomy of the Saudi Arabian Economy*

Table 2.3: Aramco proven reserves of crude oil and crude oil production*

	Aramco proven reserves (10^9 bbl)	Increase in reserves (10^9 bbl)	Production (Total) (10^9 bbl)	Rate of discovery (%)	Cumulative production (10^9 bbl)	Reserve production ratio (years)
1951	12		0.28		1	43
1952	16	4	0.30	25	1.3	53
1953	28	12	0.31	43	1.6	91
1954	36	8	0.35	22	2	103
1955	37	1	0.36	3	2.3	104
1956	40	3	0.37	7.5	2.7	109
1957	45	5	0.38	11	3.1	120
1958	47	2	0.39	4	3.4	122
1959	50	3	0.42	6	3.9	119
1960	46	−4	0.48	−	4.3	96
1961	50	4	0.54	8	4.9	93
1962	60	10	0.60	17	5.5	100
1963	61	1	0.65	2	6.1	94
1964	62	1	0.70	2	6.8	89
1965	67	5	0.80	7.5	7.6	83
1966	78	11	0.95	14	8.6	82
1967	80	2	1.0	2.5	9.6	78
1968	88	8	1.1	9	10.7	79
1969	89	1	1.2	1	11.9	76
1970	88	−1	1.4	−	13.3	63
1971	90	2	1.7	2	15.0	52
1972	93	3	2.2	3	17.2	42
1973	97	4	2.8	4	20.0	35
1974	103	6	3.1	6	23.1	33
1975	108	5	2.6	5	25.7	58

* Aramco probable reserves were 176 billion barrels in 1975. Total proven reserves in 1975 were 111.2 billion barrels.

Sources: OPEC, Aramco.

The Oil Sector

1975 annual report says 'as in every year since Aramco's commercial oil operations began in 1938, the company last year added to Saudi Arabia's known hydrocarbon reserves an amount greater than the quantity of crude oil taken out of the ground. Exploration and development resulted in an increase in proven reserves of 4.4 billion barrels, or nearly twice the amount of crude oil produced during the year'. Therefore, there is a second, positive loop that links the reserves and the discovery rate (Figure 2.2). The discovery rate is assumed to be a variable proportion of the reserves and this proportion is supposed to be a non-linear, decreasing function of cumulative production (Figure 2.1).

Figure 2.1: Rate of Discovery of New Petroleum Reserves

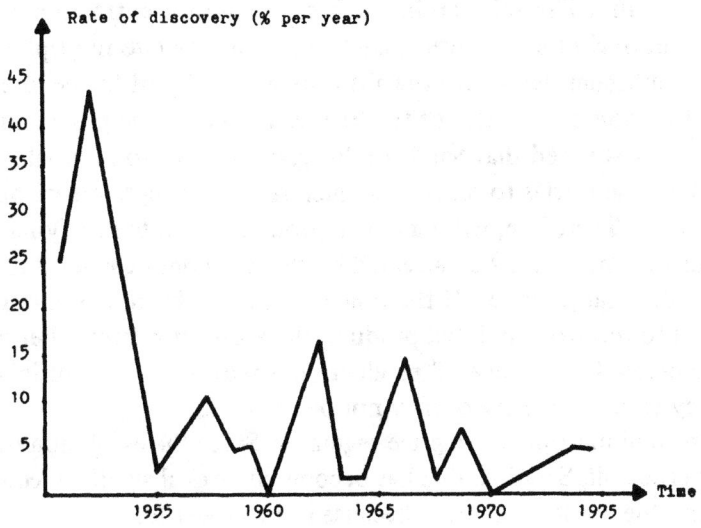

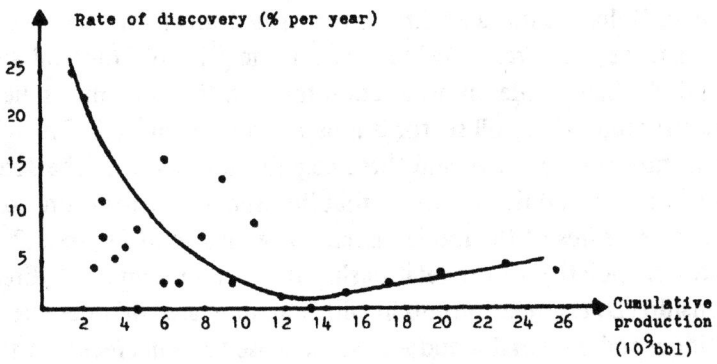

Crude oil is produced for export and domestic usage. Domestic usage of crude oil by the non-oil sector is related to the volume of non-oil production through the energy-output ratio. This variable indicates the quantity of crude oil that the economy consumes for each riyal of non-oil production. The energy-output ratio is supposed to decrease as productive capital per worker rises. This relationship means that, as productive capital accumulates, the economy becomes more efficient in the use of the factors of production.

Production for export results from complex policy decisions that involve technical, domestic and international factors. The long-term, technical aspects of crude-oil production are represented by a non-linear relationship between the extraction rate and the number of years of crude oil supply corresponding to this extraction rate. In other words, production for export is supposed to decrease with the reserve production ratio. This relationship defines the normal extraction rate. This normal rate, however, may be modified by two multipliers. The first multiplier deals with the absorptive capacity of the economy and is a function of the ratio of the financial assets to the gross national product. It is assumed that Saudi Arabia gives priority to internal accumulation and tries to recycle as much revenue as possible within the economy. Therefore, willingness to produce at a rate satisfying the consuming countries may be affected by the kingdom's capacity to absorb additional revenues. If the financial reserves become too large compared to the gross national product, the absorption multiplier may decrease below 1 and crude oil production is reduced. This multiplier is a policy variable. It may or may not be activated.

The second multiplier is a price regulator. Since the escalation of the price of crude oil, Saudi Arabia has become of critical significance to OPEC and the world oil market because of its power to affect the petroleum prices through its ability and willingness to produce at a rate far higher than its development needs call for. The recent OPEC meeting in Doha has unquestionably confirmed this fact. There consequently exists a relationship between the price of crude oil and the Saudi Arabian crude oil production through the price multiplier.

The structure of the oil sector is illustrated in Figure 2.2. The diagram shows one positive and three negative loops within the substructure and two additional loops that link the oil substructure to other substructures of the model. Each arrow shown in Figure 2.2 indicates the polarity of the relationship that is represented. A direct relationship (D) is a relationship in which an increase (or a decrease) in the independent variable induces an increase (or a decrease) in the

The Oil Sector

dependent variable. An inverse relationship (I) is a relationship in which an increase (or a decrease) in the independent variable induces a decrease (or an increase) in the dependent variable. A loop is positive if it includes an even number of inverse relationships. A loop is negative if this number is odd.

The major variable of the oil sector is the level of reserves, the value of which depends upon the dominant loops. Table 2.1 indicates that in the past the positive loop of the oil substructure has been constantly dominant. This trend may, however, rapidly reverse in the future as a result of both the long-term decrease in the discovery rate and the future increase in crude oil production. Crude oil production

Figure 2.2: Structural Representation of the Oil Sector

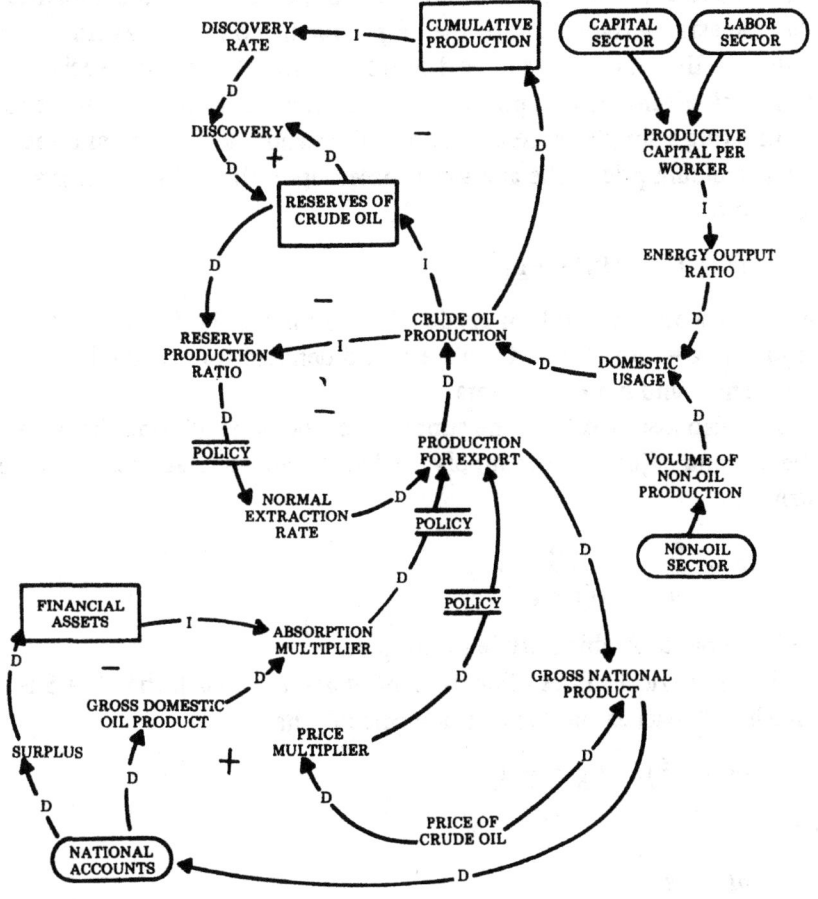

is partly controlled by the two additional loops shown in Figure 2.2 and by the price multiplier. Also important is the domestic usage of crude oil determined by the volume of non-oil production. Since crude oil production is a significant variable within the oil substructure and directly affects the level of crude oil reserves, it can be seen that the behaviour of the oil sector can be highly influenced by the behaviour of the rest of the economic system through the policy variables previously analyzed. It is also possible that these policy variables are kept inactive. In this case, the behaviour of the oil sector only results from its internal structure.

The Price of Crude Oil

The analysis of the price of crude oil is complex. It involves such elements as the world demand for crude oil, OPEC, the oil companies, the domestic development of the oil-producing countries, world inflation, the search for and cost of oil substitutes and other social, technical, economic and political factors. The model confines itself to considering a simple representation of the major elements regulating the petroleum price. The analysis is based upon the following demand function:

$$D = (a - bP)(1 + g)^t$$

with D = world demand for crude oil to Saudi Arabia, P = price of crude oil, g = rate of growth in the world demand for crude oil, t = time, and a and b are constants.

It is also assumed that, the supply of crude oil regulating the market, the demand adjusts to the supply so that the above relationship can be written:

$$P = \frac{a}{b} - \frac{S}{b(1+g)^t}$$

with S = Saudi Arabian crude oil supply.

The numerical values of coefficients a and b are such that $D = S$ is nil when P reaches the substitution price $\bar{P}$, that is

$$(a - b\bar{P})(1 + g)^t = 0$$

or

$$b\bar{P} = a$$

and the rate of growth of the world demand for crude oil to Saudi Arabia, g, is supposed to decrease when the price of crude oil

The Oil Sector

approaches the substitution price $\bar{P}$,

$$g = f(P) \text{ with } f' < 0.$$

Such a formulation implies that the price of crude oil is determined by three elements: the rate of growth of the world demand for crude oil, Saudi Arabia's production policy and the substitution price. The assumed value of the substitution price is particularly important because it defines coefficients a and b. The choice of a relevant substitution price must be based upon the most recent evaluations of the global cost of possible substitutes and must take into consideration the fact that crude oil is irreplaceable in several sectors such as petrochemical industries. Also important is the fact that, in a long-term perspective, the substitution price is variable.

Estimates of production costs for alternative energy sources have risen rapidly. Table 2.4 gives 1976 estimates for the five alternative sources closest to possible profitable commercialization. It is interesting to remember that in 1974 evaluations of the substitution price for crude oil were generally varying between US $4 and US $15 a barrel. It became clear later that the costs of alternative sources had been systematically under-evaluated, that the industrialized countries could not produce cheaper energy than the US $11 OPEC crude oil and had therefore significantly to revise their estimated import requirements.

On the basis of Table 2.4, the model assumes that the present substitution price for crude oil is US $30 a barrel. Assuming an initial crude oil production for export of 3,200 million barrels and an initial price of US $12.4 a barrel, coefficients a and b are the solution of the following system of equations:

$$3200 = a - 12.4b$$
$$a = 30b$$

that is

$$a = 5454 \qquad b = 181.8$$

Both a and b are evaluated in millions of barrels per year. Coefficient a is the maximum world demand for crude oil to Saudi Arabia and coefficient b the decrease in world demand per additional dollar in crude oil price. The ratio a/b is the substitution price. If a and b are kept constant, the price of crude oil increases when demand grows faster than supply and decreases when supply grows faster than demand. For example, with a constant production rate and a five per

Table 2.4: Cost of alternative Energy Sources

Alternative energy sources	Estimated price US $ per barrel
Oil from tar sands	27
Oil from shale	24
Coal gazification	24
Coal liquefaction	24
Methanol	24

Source: *Arab Oil and Gas*, 1 October 1976.

cent annual growth rate of the world demand, the price of crude oil reaches US $21.5 a barrel in 1990. If the price is to be kept at its 1976 level of US $12.4 a barrel, a five per cent annual rate of growth of the world demand requires a production of 18.2 million barrels per day in 1990. This simple example shows why a substantial increase in the price of crude oil in the near future is more and more considered a certainty by petroleum experts.

In the long term, the substitution price is affected by technical changes that might cut the cost of alternative energy sources and by the rate of inflation that makes technological developments more expensive. If the net rate of inflation, i.e. the difference between the rate of technical progress and the rate of inflation, is a low two per cent per year, a US $30 substitution price in 1976 is equivalent to US $49 twenty-four years later. If this net rate is four per cent a year, the substitution price rises to US $80 in year 2000. It should be added that petroleum experts are not overconfident about improved technology. According to Dr M.L. Slim Sharrah, Senior Vice-President of Continental Oil Company, 'improved technology will probably provide only slight improvement in the economics. Furthermore, lower raw material costs, capital requirements, or operating costs seem unlikely in the future'.

Table 2.5 shows the changes in the numerical value of coefficients a and b implied by higher substitution prices. Simulation experiments with the model will, on the basis of this table, consider both variable and constant substitution prices.

The connection of the price substructure to the first substructure of the model creates two additional feedback loops (Figure 2.3) that are both negative. The first loop depends upon policy decisions and may be kept inactive. The second loop depends upon the price elasticity of

The Oil Sector

Table 2.5: Effect of Higher Substitution Prices on Coefficients a and b

Substitution price (US $ per barrel)	Coefficient a (million bbl/year)	Coefficient b (million bbl/year)
60	4,032	67.2
55	4,130.5	75.1
50	4,255	85.1
45	4,419	98.2
40	4,636	115.9
35	4,956	141.6
30	5,454	181.8

Figure 2.3: The Regulation of the Price of Crude Oil

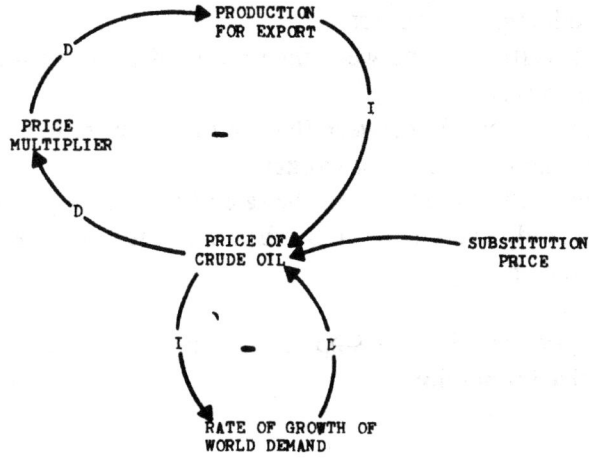

the world demand for crude oil to Saudi Arabia. Both loops tend to reduce the price through increases in the supply of crude oil.

Quantification of the Non-Linear Relationships in the Oil Sector

Several relationships of the oil sector are non-linear. Often, these relationships cannot be defined by an equation and are quantified through numerical tables (function TABLE) that constitute linear approximations of the postulated non-linear relationships. These numerical tables deal with policy decisions as well as behavioural or structural changes. It is impossible to foresee or anticipate such decisions

decisions and changes. It is however possible to set up a series of logical assumptions about these decisions and changes and to evaluate clearly, through the simulation model, their impact and consequences. This method is called scenario analysis. A scenario is a set of assumptions about economic and social changes that seem probable or possible in the future. Of course, none of these alternative scenarios will actually correspond to the real facts in the future, but, if the simulation experiments are correctly defined, it is probable that the reality will stand somewhere among the simulated futures.

There are six non-linear relationships to define in the oil sector:

1. the relationship between the discovery rate and cumulative crude oil production;
2. the relationship between the normal extraction rate and the reserve production ratio;
3. the relationship between the absorption multiplier and production for export;
4. the relationship between the price multiplier and production for export;
5. the relationship between the energy output ratio and productive capital per worker;
6. the relationship between the rate of growth of the world demand for crude oil to Saudi Arabia and the price of crude oil.

Figure 2.4: Assumed Relationship between the Discovery Rate and Cumulative Production

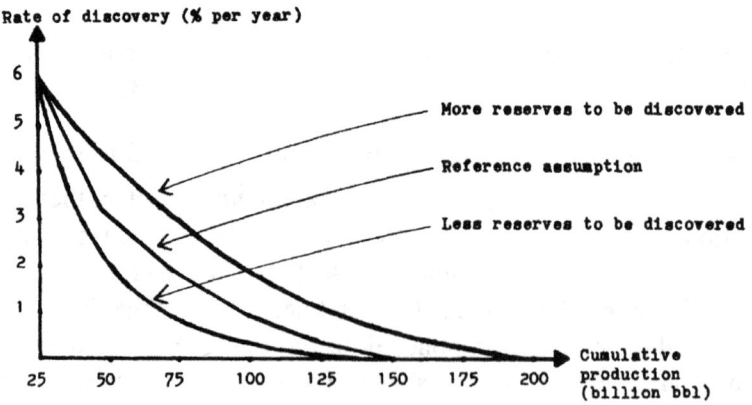

The Oil Sector

The first relationship is approximated from past data in Figure 2.1. It is assumed that similar changes will take place in the future (Figure 2.4), the average slope of the relationship being defined in accordance with the fact that Saudi Arabia's probable crude oil reserves are close to 200 billion barrels and that possible reserves might be as high as 300 billion barrels.

The numerical table corresponding to the diagram of Figure 2.4 is:

Discovery rate	Cumulative production
6	25
3.2	50
1.8	75
0.9	100
0.3	125
0	150

The numerical values that are not defined by the table are computed by linear interpolation.

The second, third and fourth relationships deal with policy decisions. Therefore, several alternative strategies can be simulated (Figure 2.5). There are three basic alternatives. Either Saudi Arabia strictly limits its production to what its development needs call for, which implies an approximate daily production of four to eight million barrels, a limited accumulation of financial reserves and no policy control on the price through increases in production (assumption A in Figure 2.5); or Saudi Arabia meets the world demand, which implies a daily production of at least eight to nine million barrels presently and may be as much as twenty million barrels in the future, no control on the accumulation of financial assets and a possible regulation of the crude oil price through the price multiplier (assumption B in Figure 2.5); or, at last, Saudi Arabia opts for a compromise with more or less emphasis on the first or the second basic strategy. In each case, however, Saudi Arabia has to secure enough crude-oil supply to meet future domestic requirements. The implications of each policy decision are extremely important at both the national and the international level. These implications are analyzed in detail in the second part of this book.

The average value of the energy output ratio is given in Table 2.6. As productive capital per worker accumulates, this coefficient is supposed either to constant or to moderately decrease (Figure 2.6).

Figure 2.5: The Policy Decisions Regulating the Oil Sector

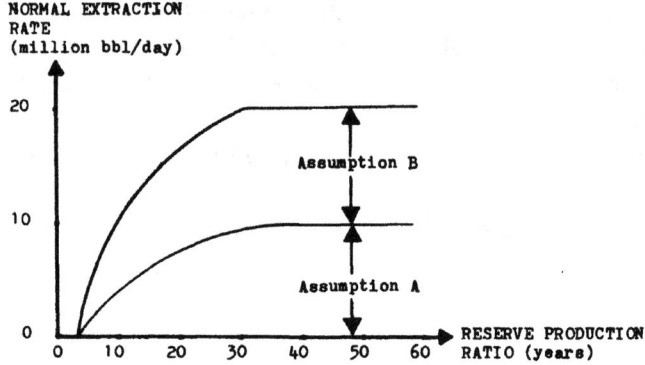

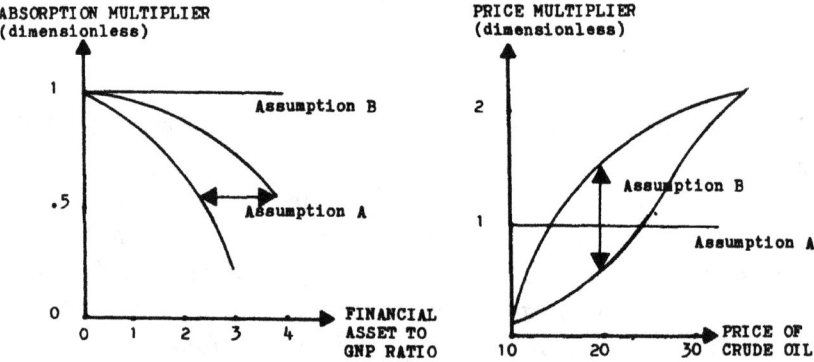

Table 2.6: Changes in the Energy Output Ratio, 1968–1974

	Gross domestic product non-oil sector (million SR)	Local consumption of petroleum products (million bbl)	Energy-output ratio (average: 0.00167)
1968	7,764	13.3	0.00171
1969	8,705	14.2	0.00163
1970	9,293	15.5	0.00167
1971	10,340	17.2	0.00166
1972	11,325	20.0	0.00177
1973	14,267	24.9	0.00175
1974	21,245	32.0	0.00151
1975	28,485	n.a.	n.a.

Source: Saudi Arabian Monetary Agency.

The Oil Sector

The effect of the energy-output ratio on the overall behaviour of the model is limited. An average growth rate of the gross domestic non-oil product of seven per cent a year until, for example, year 2000 implies, with a constant energy-output ratio, a domestic consumption of less than 0.8 million barrels per day this year.

Figure 2.6: Assumed Changes in the Energy-Output Ratio

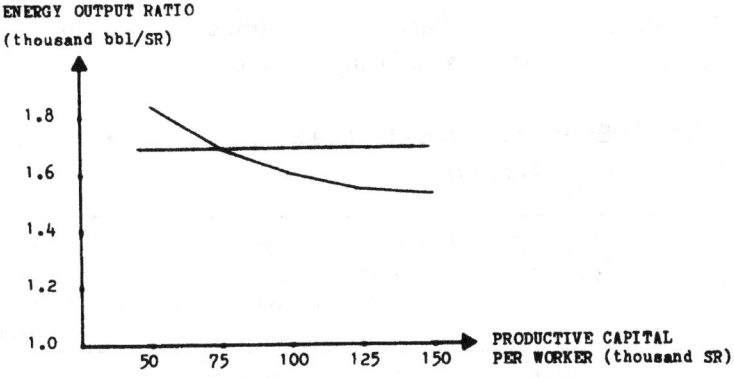

Table 2.7: Oil Consumption in Europe (million bbl/day)

	1974	1975	1976
Oil consumption	10.4	9.4	10
Growth rate	−6%	−9%	6%

The last non-linear relationship of the oil sector deals with the growth of the world oil demand to Saudi Arabia. From 1950 to 1970, the free-world primary consumption of crude oil grew at an average rate of eight per cent per year from approximately eight million barrels per day in 1950 to forty million in 1970. Three years later, in 1973, the top ten consuming countries consumed forty-three million barrels per day, that is, more than the 1970 world consumption. After the 1973 increase in the price of crude oil, the world consumption temporarily decreased — the consumption of the top ten consuming countries was respectively 41.6 and 38.9 million barrels daily in 1974 and 1975 — but 1976 consumption was up again. The world consumption of crude oil has grown by 7.6 per cent in 1976 to 54.6 million barrels per day and the European consumption by 6 per cent (see Table 2.7).

According to 1974 estimates, the free world primary demand for crude oil might reach eighty-eight million barrels per day in 1985, and according to 1976 estimates, the free world might import as much as thirty-three million barrels per day from the OPEC countries by mid-1977. At that rate, OPEC should produce between thirty-seven and thirty-nine million barrels per day in 1980 to meet the world demand. In September 1976, OPEC production was 29.3 million barrels per day for a theoretical production capacity of 38.8 million barrels daily (Table 2.8). However, only thirty to thirty-five per cent of the theoretical spare capacity can actually generate increases in production

Table 2.8: OPEC Production and Production Capacity, September 1976 (millions of barrels daily)

	Production capacity	Actual production	Utilization rate of the capacity	Theoretical spare capacity	Estimated 1977 production capacity
Saudi Arabia	11.8	8.34	71%	3.46	12.6
Iran	6.6	5.64	85%	0.96	6.6
Kuwait	3.3	1.89	57%	1.41	3.3
Iraq	2.8	1.99	71%	0.81	3.1
Venezuela	2.75	2.27	83%	0.48	3.0
Nigeria	2.7	2.03	75%	0.67	2.7
Libya	2.5	1.89	76%	0.61	2.5
UAE	2.4	1.91	80%	0.49	2.5
Indonesia	1.75	1.49	85%	0.26	1.8
Algeria	1.1	0.96	87%	0.14	1.1
Qatar	0.65	0.49	75%	0.16	0.65
Gabon	0.25	0.21	84%	0.04	0.25
Equator	0.22	0.18	82%	0.04	0.22
TOTAL	38.82	29.29	75%	9.53	40.32

Source: Arab Oil and Gas.

and most of the increase in capacity expected in 1977 will be in Saudi Arabia which might raise its production up to 11.9 million barrels per day, that is, a thirty-five per cent increase from the production ceiling of 8.8 million barrels per day. Such an increase is aimed at both meeting the 1977 world demand and neutralizing the price increase decided by eleven OPEC countries in Doha. The 'reserve capacity'

The Oil Sector

kept by Saudi Arabia for use 'only in special circumstances' is three million barrels per day. As a result, the normal 1977 extraction rate would be 8.9 million barrels per day with a 1.34 price multiplier which may be expected to drop back to 1 with the settlement of OPEC temporary division. However, a normal extraction rate of 8.9 million barrels per day does not seem sufficient to meet the projected world demand after 1977 and it is estimated that Saudi Arabia will have to authorize a ten million barrel per day production level. One should also consider that, in a longer range, Saudi Arabia might have to compensate the decrease in production of countries with a present low level of reserves.

If, according to the above analysis, it is assumed that, in order to meet the world demand, Saudi Arabia will gradually increase its normal extraction rate from 8.4 million barrels per day in mid-1977 to, say, 10 in 1980, the corresponding average annual rate of growth of the world oil demand to the kingdom is 5.1 per cent. This rather conservative assumption, supplemented by the hypothesis that the world demand will remain relatively inelastic to the price of crude oil, leads to Figure 2.7.

Figure 2.7: Assumed Changes in the Rate of Growth of the World Oil Demand to Saudi Arabia

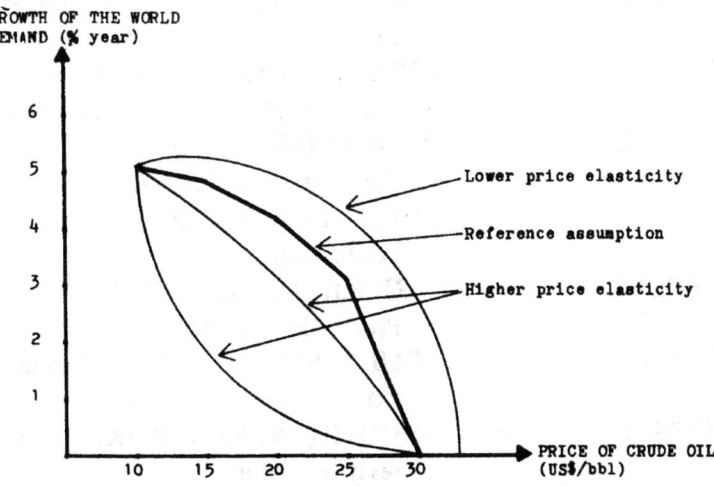

The Adjustment Delays of the Substructure

Many economic relationships are not instantaneous. For example, several years may separate the decision to invest from the actual acquisition of capital goods. The model takes this fact into consideration through DELAY functions that picture the delays in material flows such as goods into an inventory or men into the labour force. Delays may either stabilize the behaviour of a system or generate unsteadiness. The impact of a material delay depends upon its order and its intensity. The order of a material delay affects the response type of the delayed variable to a given input. The velocity of a material delay affects the rapidity of this response.

Another type of delay is the information delay. Information delays are exponential smooth functions (function SMOOTH) which picture the fact that information does not perfectly circulate within a system. Decisions are not taken according to the actual state of the system, which is never perfectly known by the decision makers, but according to the decision makers' perception of this state. As material delays, information delays are characterized by their order and their velocity.

There are six SMOOTH functions in the oil substructure that are shown in Figure 2.8. This diagram also indicates the TABLE functions of the substructure.

The Equations of the Substructure

The oil sector is mathematically described by the following seventeen equations. A detailed listing of the simulation programme is given in Appendix 1 and the variables of the model are defined in Appendix 2.

ORES.K	=	ORES.J + (DT)(DISCO.JK − COP.JK) Reserves of crude oil	(1)
DISCO.KL	=	(DIRAT.K)(ORES.K) Discoveries	(2)
DIRAT.K	=	TABLE(ACOP.K) Discovery rate	(3)
ACOP.K	=	ACOP.J + (DT)(COP.JK) Cumulative production	(4)
COP.KL	=	COPEX.K + DOMUS.K Crude-oil production	(5)
COPEX.K	=	(PRN.K)(ACMUL.K)(OPMUL.K) Production for export	(6)
PRN.K	=	(TABLE(SRPR.K))(365) Normal extraction rate (policy)	(7)
SRPR.K	=	SMOOTH(ORES.K/COP.JK) Smoothed reserve production ratio	(8)

The Oil Sector

Figure 2.8: Tables and Delays in the Oil Substructure

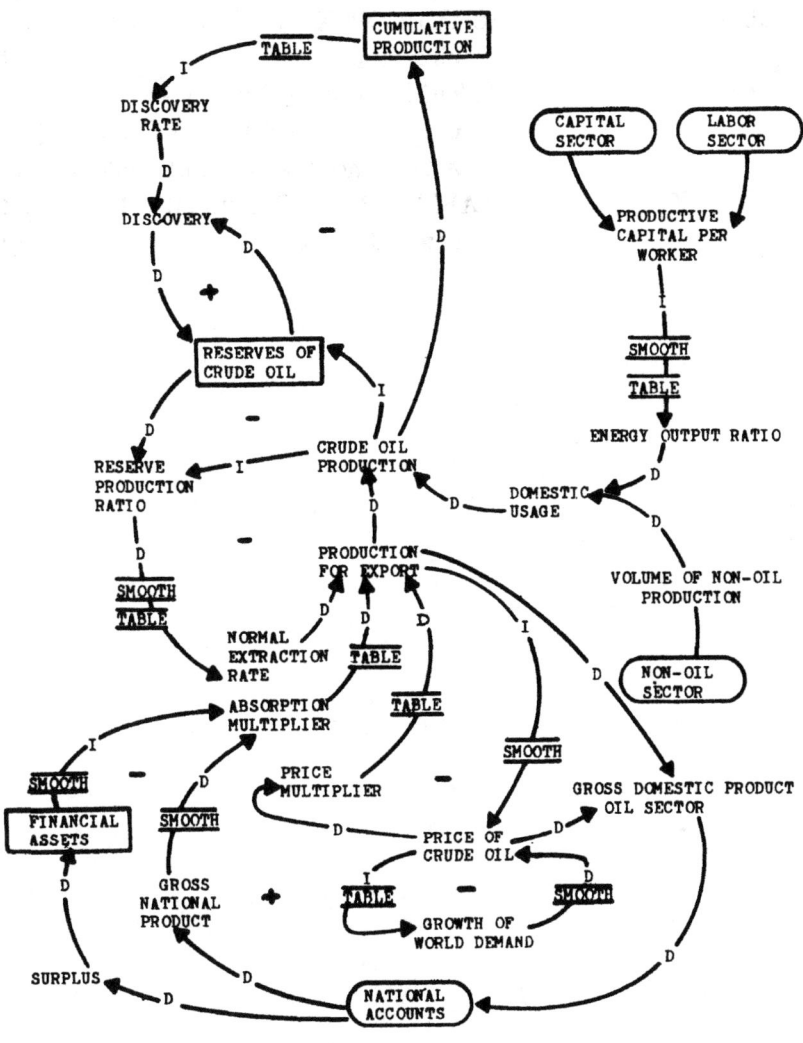

ACMUL.K	=	TABLE(SAOR.K) Absorption multiplier (policy)	(9)
SAOR.K	=	SMOOTH(FINAS.K/GNP.K) Smoothed ratio of financial assets to GNP	(10)
OPMUL.K	=	TABLE (SP.K) Price multiplier	(11)
DOMUS.K	=	(EOR.K)(VNOP.JK) Domestic usage	(12)
EOR.K	=	TABLE(CAPWO.K) Energy output ratio	(13)

CAPWO.K	=	SMOOTH(CAP.K/TLF.K) Smoothed capital per worker (14)
GDPOIL.K	=	(SP.K)(COPEX.K)(ERSR) GDP oil sector (15)
SP.K	=	SMOOTH([MWD/DWDA] − COPEX.K/[DWDA$(1 + $RGWD.K$)^t$] $\times$ t) Smoothed price of crude oil (16)
RGWD.K	=	TABLE(SP.K) Growth rate of the world demand for oil (17)

3 THE NON-OIL SECTOR

The Production Function

The model aggregates into a single substructure and treats as a unique sector all economic activities giving rise to the gross domestic non-oil product. As opposed to the oil substructure, the non-oil substructure explicitly considers the mechanism of production through a production function. It is assumed that non-oil production results from the combination of two factors of production, labour and capital, and that the mechanism of production is described by the following equations:

VNOP.KL = MIN (PCAP.K, PCLAB.K)   Volume of non-oil production (value added)
PCAP.K = CAP.K/COR.K   Production capacity from capital
PCLAB.K = PCSL.K + PCFL.K   Production capacity from labour
PCSL.K = (SLF.K)(NHW)/SLOR.K   Production capacity from Saudi labour
PCFL.K = (FLF.K)(NHW)/FLOR.K   Production capacity from foreign labour

with

CAP = total productive capital
COR = capital output ratio
FLF = foreign labour force
FLOR = foreign labour output ratio
NHW = number of man hours per year
SLF = Saudi labour force
SLOR = Saudi labour output ratio

The formulation of the production function implies that appropriate amounts of each factor must be supplied by the economic system. In other words, if there exists a shortage or a surplus in production capacity from a given factor, the actual level of production is fixed by the less abundant factor and the other factor is underemployed. In equation form, this is:

VNOP = PCAP = PCLAB if PCAP = PCLAB
VNOP = PCAP if PCAP < PCLAB
VNOP = PCLAB if PCLAB > PCAP

The advantage of this type of production function is that it is not assumed that the supply of other factors of production such as labour or entrepreneurship is also forthcoming as capital usage is increased. In this respect, the production function takes into account the fact that, in Saudi Arabia, the labour force is one of the major constraints in the process of economic development. It is however assumed, through the definition of the labour-output ratios, that capital can substitute for labour (see Chapter 4).

The Structure of the Non-Oil Sector

The structure of the non-oil sector is based upon three major flows: the flow of produced and imported goods into the inventory, the flow of orders to the sector, and the flow of shipments to the various demanders. The dynamic equilibrium of the sector depends upon the capacity of the economic system to synchronize these flows correctly.

The accumulation of goods into the inventory permits the non-oil sector to absorb more easily the fluctuations of demand. This accumulation results from domestic production and imports which depend upon the discrepancy between desired and actual non-oil production. Orders to the non-oil sector are generated by the various demand flows (consumer demand and investment demand) and accumulate into levels of unfilled orders. These levels, together with the inventory level, are decreased by the shipments sent to both consumers and investors. Shipment flows are determined by both the levels of unfilled orders and delays filling orders. These delays are defined as a function of the ratio between the inventory level and the corresponding demand flow.

In addition to this mechanism, there is a dynamic adjustment of actual non-oil production to desired production. Desired production is determined by both the total demand to the non-oil sector and the inventory adjustment mechanism. This mechanism is also a dynamic adjustment: the adjustment of actual inventory to desired inventory. Desired inventory is assumed to be a variable proportion of total shipments sent, this proportion being determined by the smoothed rate of growth of the shipment flows. Desired production is an important variable because it determines the demand for factors of production and the production level.

The Non-Oil Sector

The structure of the non-oil sector is represented in Figure 3.1. The diagram shows the three negative loops that tend to decrease the levels of unfilled orders. The positive loops on these levels are generated from outside the substructure and involve the various demand flows shown in Figure 3.1. The diagram also shows three additional

Figure 3.1: Structure of the Non-Oil Sector

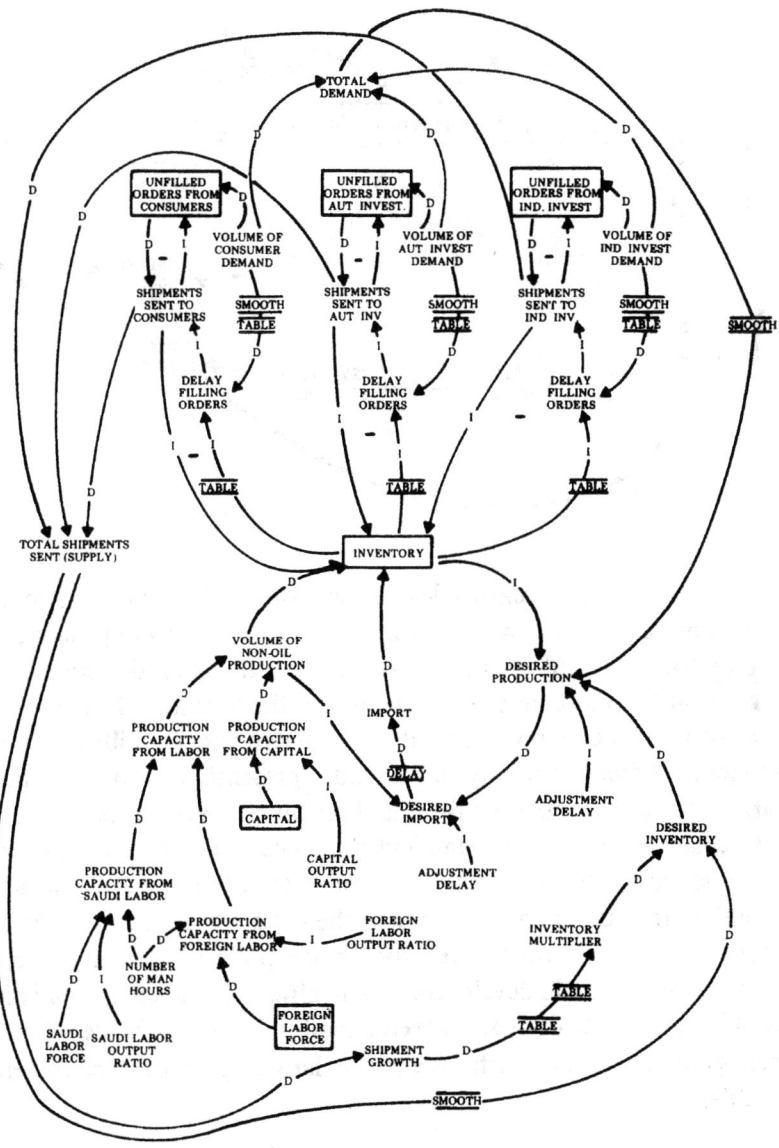

negative loops that tend to decrease the inventory level through the various shipment flows. These loops connect the inventory level to the levels of unfilled orders and link the non-oil substructure to the rest of the economic system. The shipment flows also positively affect the inventory level through the following information network that represents part of the inventory adjustment mechanism:

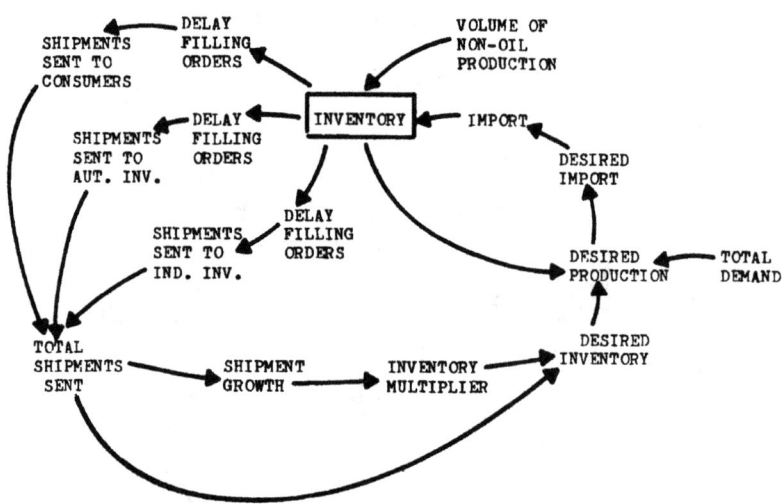

In addition, the inventory level is positively affected by the volume of non-oil production, which results from the production process, and by total demand. As these variables directly and indirectly involve all the substructures of the model, the inventory level is a very significant economic indicator of the dynamic equilibrium of the economy. Adjusting supply to demand is presently one of the major targets of the regulation of the Saudi Arabian economy. Large discrepancies between demand and supply capacity significantly increase the delays in filling orders, generate bottlenecks and sustain inflation. Inflation might either help the system to achieve equilibrium again or, on the contrary, intensify the disequilibrium. In any case, the cost of the economic development is significantly increased. As Saudi Arabia pays for its domestic development in barrels of crude oil, a persistent inflation constitutes a particularly important development problem.

Quantification of the Non-Linear Relationships

There are three non-linear relationships to quantify in the non-oil substructure. The first relationship (Figure 3.2) links the delay filling orders from consumers to the ratio of the inventory level to the volume of consumer demand. As the size of the inventory gets smaller relative to the ordering rate, the delivery delay gets larger. When the inventory

Figure 3.2: Assumed Relationship between the Delay in Filling Orders from Consumers and the Inventory to Consumer Demand Ratio

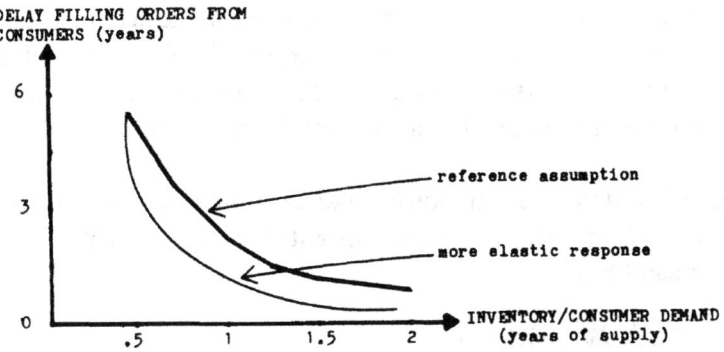

is large enough, the sector is able to deliver more than the current ordering rate and to catch up with previous unfilled orders. A similar relationship characterizes the investment process (Figure 3.3). However, the delays in filling orders from investors are significantly larger than the delay in filling orders from consumers. The reason is that the production of several types of investment goods such as infrastructure investments or sophisticated industrial equipment cannot obviously be implemented before corresponding orders have been received. As Saudi Arabia is planning to allocate large amounts of financial resources to infrastructural investments, the relationship has to take into account the physical delay between investment demand and capital acquisition. As the model is aggregated and does not differentiate the various investment types, the value of the delays in filling orders from investors results from the combined influence of the production delay and the inventory delay.

The relationships shown in Figures 3.2 and 3.3 are important. They determine the capacity of the system to meet demand and affect the rate of inflation.

The third non-linear relationship of the non-oil substructure is the relationship between the inventory multiplier and the growth rate of the shipment flows (Figure 3.4). This relationship may be kept constant. In this case, it is assumed that the management of the inventory is not affected by the variations in shipment flows. A variable relationship implies that the desired size of the inventory gets smaller as sales moderate.

The inventory multiplier is another important variable. It directly affects desired inventory which, together with total demand, determines the desired volume of non-oil production, the orders for factors of production and the actual volume of non-oil production (Figure 3.1). A large inventory multiplier consequently leads the economy to allocate more financial resources to domestic development and modifies the long-term structural evolution of the economy through the reinforcement of internal accumulation to the detriment of the

Figure 3.3: Assumed Relationship between the Delays in Filling Orders from Investors and the Inventory to Investment Demand Ratios

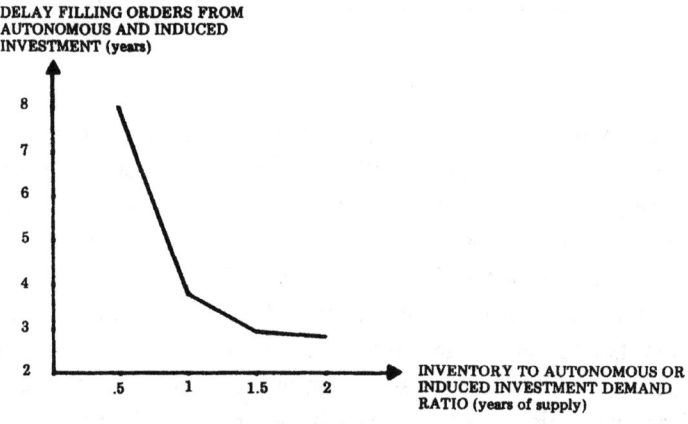

Figure 3.4: Assumed Relationship between the Inventory Multiplier and the Growth Rate of Shipment Flows

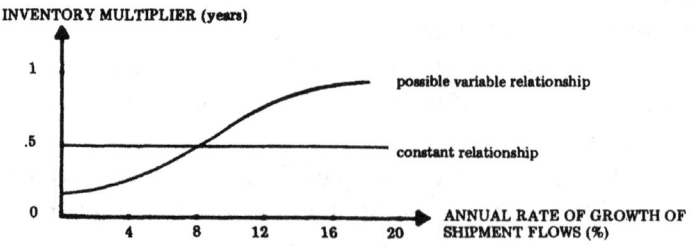

The Non-Oil Sector 45

financial assets. A large inventory multiplier also stimulates demand and may increase the inflation rate.

The Equations of the Substructure

The non-oil substructure is composed of the following twenty-four equations:

UFOC.K	= UFOC.J + (DT)(VCDEM.JK − SSC.JK) Unfilled orders from consumers	(18)
SSC.KL	= UFOC.K/DFOC.K Shipments sent to consumers	(19)
DFOC.K	= TABLE(STOCK.K/SCDEM.K) Delay filling orders (consumers)	(20)
UFOAI.K	= UFOAI.J + (DT)(VAINV.JK − SSAI.JK) Unfilled orders from aut. investment	(21)
SSAI.KL	= UFOAI.K/DFOAI.K Shipments sent to aut. investment	(22)
DFOAI.K	= TABLE(STOCK.K/SAIDEM.K) Delay filling orders (aut. inv.)	(23)
UFOII.K	= UFOII.J + (DT)(IINV.JK − SSII.JK) Unfilled orders from induced invest.	(24)
SSII.KL	= UFOII.K/DFOII.K Shipments sent to induced investment	(25)
DFOII.K	= TABLE(STOCK.K/SIIDEM.K) Delay in filling orders (ind. inv.)	(26)
STOCK.K	= STOCK.J + (DT)(VNOP.JK + IMPORT.JK − SSC.JK − SSAI.JK − SSII.JK) Inventory level	(27)
VNOP.KL	= MIN(PCAP.K, PCLAB.K) Volume of non-oil production	(28)
PCAP.K	= CAP.K/COR.K Production capacity from capital	(29)
PCLAB.K	= PCSL.K + PCFL.K Production capacity from labour	(30)
PCSL.K	= (SLF.K)(NHW)/SLOR.K Production capacity from Saudi labour	(31)
PCFL.K	= (FLF.K)(NHW)/FLOR.K Production capacity from foreign labour	(32)
IMPORT.KL	= DELAY(DESIMP.K) Imports	(33)
DESIMP.K	= (DVNOP.K − VNOP.JK)/AD Desired imports	(34)

DVNOP.K	= STDEM.K + (DSTOCK.K − STOCK.K)/ADD	
	Desired volume of non-oil production	(35)
DSTOCK.K	= (STM.K)(STSS.K) Desired inventory	(36)
STM.K	= TABLE(SSG.K) Inventory multiplier	(37)
SG.K	= $\dfrac{TSS.K - TSS.J}{(TTS.J)(DT)}$ Shipment growth	(38)
STSS.K	= SMOOTH(TSS.K) Smoothed shipments	(39)
SSG.K	= SMOOTH(SG.K) Smoothed shipment growth	(40)
TSS.K	= SSC.JK + SSAU.JK + SSII.JK Total shipments sent	(41)

4 THE FACTORS OF PRODUCTION

In the non-oil sector, the production of goods and services results from appropriate combinations of the labour force and the stock of productive capital. The acquisition of labour depends upon the growth of the Saudi population, the structure of the Saudi labour force and the importation of foreign labour. The accumulation of productive capital is determined by the investment process which is controlled by governmental policy decisions and the growth of the economy.

Population and the Saudi Labour Force

The Saudi labour force is a key variable for the long-term development of the economy. The growth of the Saudi labour force depends upon such factors as the growth and the structure of the Saudi population as well as the jurisdictional organization of the labour market. A detailed analysis of these factors requires a degree of structural disaggregation that goes beyond the scope of the model. It is simply assumed that the Saudi labour force is an exogenous proportion of total population.

The dynamics of population growth results from the long-term changes in both the birth rate and the death rate. Figure 4.1 shows that there exists, at the world level, a structural link between the rate of birth and the gross national product per capita. The rate of death depends upon such variables as diet patterns, the dissemination of basic sanitary knowledge, preventive medicine, and the general development of medical facilities and equipment. The model summarizes these various factors through a single variable, the average wealth per capita.

The average efficiency of the Saudi labour force is measured by the Saudi labour output ratio. The model assumes that this ratio is variable and depends upon the total productive capital per capita. As capital accumulates, more services are provided to the population, particularly education and training. Also, the accumulation of productive capital generates technical progress and makes labour more efficient.

The corresponding equations are:

POP.K = POP.J + (DT)(NB.JK − ND.JK)   Saudi

Figure 4.1: Birth Rate and GNP per capita for more than 100 Countries

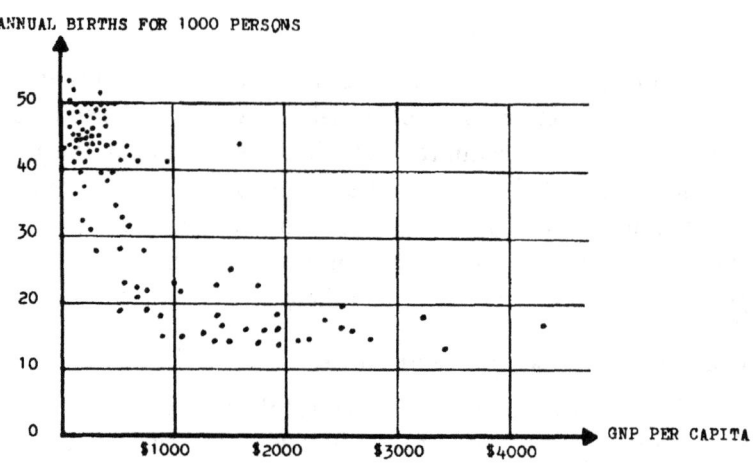

Source: *The Limits to Growth.*

		population	(42)
NB.KL	=	(BR.K)(POP.K) Number of births	(43)
BR.K	=	TABLE(SRGNPC.K) Birth rate	(44)
SRGNPC.K	=	SMOOTH($\frac{\text{GNP.K/PRIND.K}}{\text{POP.K}}$) Smoothed real GNP per capita	(45)
ND.KL	=	(DR.K)(POP.K) Number of deaths	(46)
DR.K	=	TABLE(SWPC.K) Death rate	(47)
SWPC.K	=	SMOOTH(TCAP.K/POP.K) Smoothed wealth per capita	(48)
TCAP.K	=	CAP.K + (FINAS.K/PRIND.K) Total capital	(49)
SLF.K	=	(AM.K)(POP.K) Saudi labour force	(50)
AM.K	=	TABLE(TIME.K) Activity multiplier (policy)	(51)
SLOR.K	=	TABLE(SCAPCA.K) Saudi labour output ratio	(52)
SCAPCA.K	=	SMOOTH(CAP.K/POP.K) Smoothed productive capital per capita	(53)

The Factors of Production

The relationship between the rate of birth and the real gross national product per capita (Equation 44) is deduced from the relationship shown in Figure 4.1. It is however not certain that the Saudi Arabian birth rate will, in the long-term, conform to the world standard. There exist in Saudi Arabia distinctive social, religious and psychological attitudes that might lead to different kinds of behaviour towards natality. Furthermore, the development of the kingdom requires a large population and it is probable that the government will make every effort to encourage a large birth rate. Therefore, several structural assumptions should be considered (Figure 4.2).

The relationship between the rate of death and wealth per capita (Equation 47) is shown in Figure 4.3. As wealth per capita increases, the death rate is supposed to decrease.

Figure 4.2: Assumed Relationship between Birth Rate and Real Gross National Product per capita

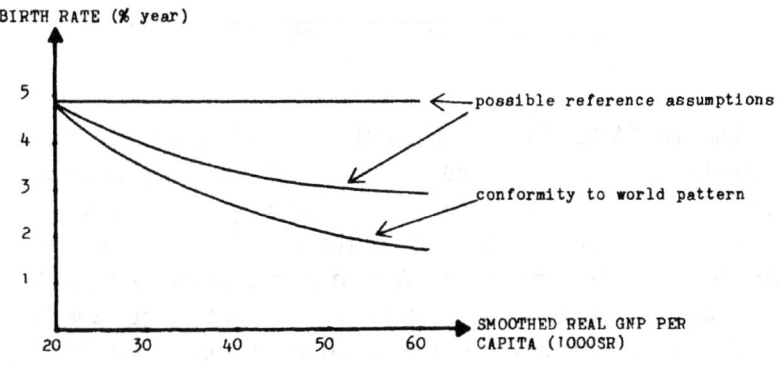

Figure 4.3: Assumed Relationship between Death Rate and Wealth per capita

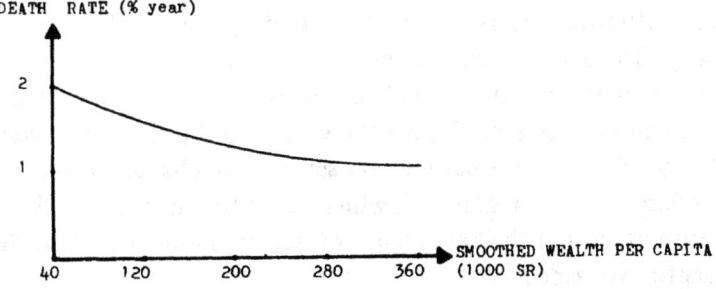

The activity multiplier (Equation 51) represents the proportion of the Saudi population constituting the Saudi labour force. The model assumes that this multiplier is exogenous and varies according to the diagram of Figure 4.4.

Figure 4.4: Assumed Changes in the Activity Multiplier

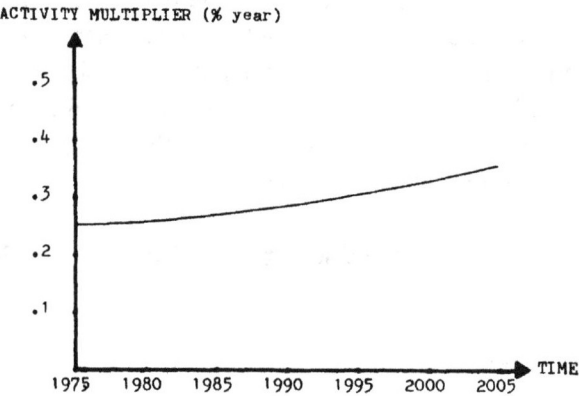

The last TABLE function (Equation 52) links the Saudi labour output ratio to the smoothed total productive capital per capita. The present value of the Saudi labour output ratio is high, which means that the average efficiency of the Saudi labour force is low. As was mentioned previously, substantial improvements in productivity are assumed to occur as capital per capita rises (Figure 4.5).

Both the quantitative and the qualitative aspects of the Saudi labour force are very important to the long-term economic development of the kingdom. A larger population provides a larger labour force and reduces the dependence of the kingdom upon foreign labour. Also, the cost of development programmes is significantly reduced when monetary leakages such as exported salaries or profits, which directly depend upon the level of foreign labour employment, are kept low. These quantitative factors are supplemented by the effects of labour efficiency. The Saudi labour output ratio acts as a multiplier that increases the contribution of the Saudi labour force to the production of goods and services even though the volume of this labour force does not change. The model is particularly sensitive to changes in the relationship shown in Figure 4.5, which tends to indicate that the qualitative aspects of the Saudi labour force are more important than the quantitative aspects.

The Factors of Production

Figure 4.5: Saudi Labour Output Ratio and Productive Capital per capita. Assumed Relationship

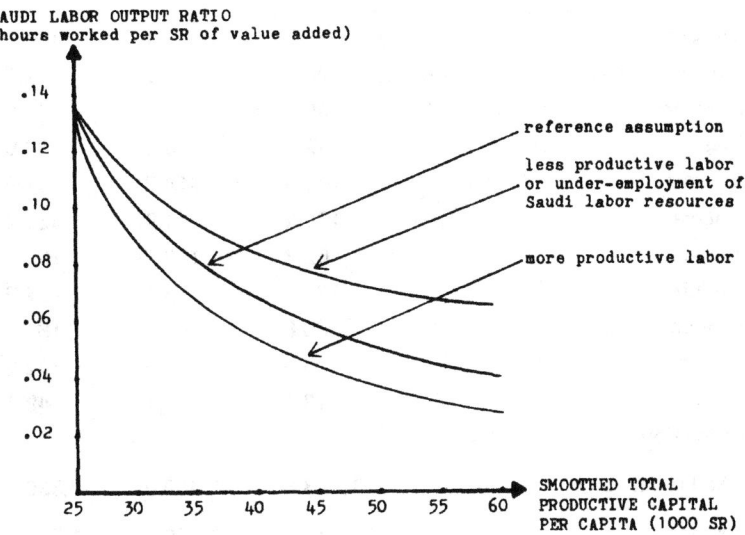

The Foreign Labour Force

Table 4.1 indicates that an essential characteristic of the Saudi Arabian economy is that indigenous labour resources are not sufficient to supply the production process with the labour resources that it needs. As a result, additional labour must be imported. The size of the foreign labour force depends upon the net acquisition of foreign labour and the average duration of foreigners' labour contracts. Foreign labour acquisition is determined by the difference between the production capacity from capital and the production capacity from labour. If the difference is positive, labour is imported. If the difference is negative, there exists a labour surplus and foreigners' labour contracts are terminated. In addition, the model assumes that the normal duration of foreigners' labour contracts is four years so that, each year, one fourth of the total foreign labour force leaves the kingdom. The corresponding equations are as follows:

$$\text{FLF.K} = \text{FLF.J} + (\text{DT})(\text{NLA.JK} - \text{RLAB.JK}) \quad \text{Foreign labour force} \quad (54)$$

$$\text{NLA.KL} = \text{DELAY}(\text{FLDE.K}) \quad \text{Net labour acquisition} \quad (55)$$

52 The Anatomy of the Saudi Arabian Economy

Table 4.1: Projected Growth in Labour Force (thousand)

Sectors	1970	1975	1980
Agriculture	445.8	426.1	395.1
Mining, oil and gas	25.7	45.6	62.1
Manufacturing	36.1	46.5	77.5
Utilities	12.2	18.3	29.5
Construction	141.5	314.2	591.9
Commerce	130.2	211.0	361.4
Transport	62.1	103.2	162.5
Community	137.5	188.4	297.9
Public administration	60.8	85.2	162.1
Education	38.5	62.5	142.2
Health	13.4	21.1	48.4
Non classified	–	77.9	–
TOTAL labour force	1,103.8	1,600.0	2,330.6
Saudis	n.a.	1,286	1,518
Non Saudis	n.a.	314	813

Source: Second Development Plan.

$$\text{FLDE.K} = \frac{(\text{PCAP.K} - \text{PCLAB.K})(\text{FLOR.K})}{\text{NHW}}$$

		Demand for foreign labour	(56)
FLOR.K	=	TABLE (CAPWO.K) Foreign labour output ratio	(57)
RLAB.KL	=	FLF.K/ADFC Returning labour	(58)
TLF.K	=	SLF.K + FLF.K Total labour force	(59)

Equation 56 is based upon the implicit assumption that all available Saudi labourers are employed in priority. This, however, does not mean that the model assumes full employment of the Saudi labour force. Potential under-employment of Saudi labour resources can be taken into consideration in the definition of the relationship determining the Saudi labour output ratio (Figure 4.5).

The average efficiency of the foreign labour force is supposed to increase as productive capital per worker accumulates (Equation 57 and Figure 4.6). It is assumed that the accumulation of productive

Factors of Production

capital is beneficial to the efficiency of both the Saudi and the foreign labour force but it is also supposed that the imported labour is fully trained.

Therefore, although the foreign labour force is assumed to be initially more efficient than the Saudi labour force increases in Saudi productivity are substantially larger.

Figure 4.6: Assumed Changes in the Foreign Labour Output Ratio

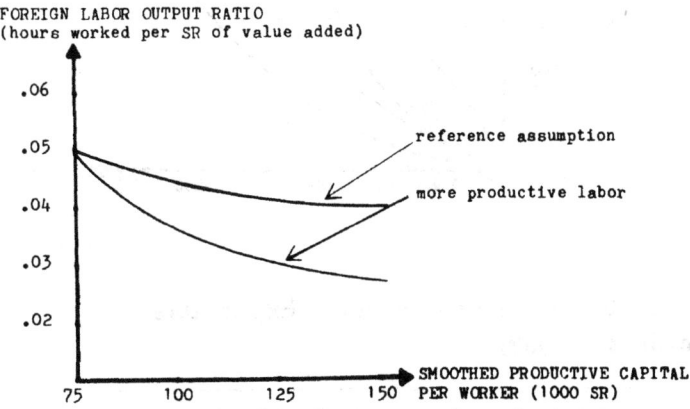

The Stock of Productive Capital

In the model, the process of capital accumulation is viewed from a dual perspective. It is assumed that decisions to invest are either autonomous, that is, independent of the state of the economic system, or induced, that is, generated by the growth in total demand and desired production.

Autonomous investments result from governmental policy decisions allocating public savings to domestic accumulation. This policy, together with the policies controlling the oil sector, is the most important in this model. Government expenditures constitute one of the major sources of economic development in the kingdom, especially when the massive required appropriations of the Second Development Plan are taken into consideration (Table 4.2). The Plan's allocated expenditure is equivalent to forty per cent of all the European Economic Community's national budgets for 1976. The model assumes that the autonomous investment demand is totally exogenous (Figure 4.7). This demand generates capital acquisitions that add to the level of productive capital.

54 The Anatomy of the Saudi Arabian Economy

Figure 4.7: Alternative Strategies of Government Spending

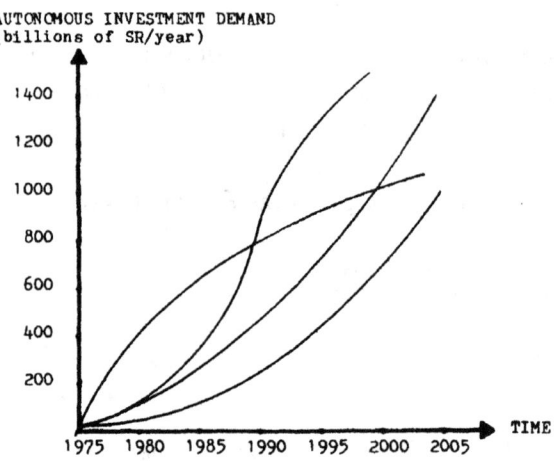

Table 4.2: Government Revenues and Expenditures
(millions of riyals)

	1947/48	1970/71	1971/72	1972/73	1973/74	1974/75	1975/76
Revenues	215	7,940	11,120	15,368	22,810	98,247	95,743
Expenditures:							
Current	n.a.	3,483	4,263	5,310	7,000	14,698	36,556
Capital	n.a.	2,273	3,378	4,178	7,150	26,397	74,379
Aid to arab countries	n.a.	662	662	660	660	4,648	n.a.
TOTAL	215	6,418	8,303	10,148	45,743	45,743	110,935
Surplus	0	1,552	2,817	5,220	8,000	52,504	−15,088

NB. The total planned expenditures of the Second (1975–1980) Development Plan are 498,200 million riyals distributed into current: 166,600 and capital : 331,600.

Sources: First National City Bank, Second Development Plan, Saudi Arabian Monetary Agency.

Factors of Production

Induced investments are determined by the gap between desired and actual capital. A positive difference means that the stock of productive capital does not meet the present needs of the economy and that additional investments are required. These investments also add to the level of productive capital. Desired capital is determined by desired production (Figure 4.11).

The capital level depreciates. The model assumes that the average depreciation rate is constant. The corresponding equations are as follows:

$$\text{CAP.K} = \text{CAP.J} + (\text{DT})(\text{ACAC.JK} + \text{ICAC.JK} - \text{CDEP.JK}) \quad \text{Productive capital} \quad (60)$$

$$\text{ACAC.KL} = \text{DELAY}(\text{SSAI.JK}) \quad \text{Autonomous capital acquisition} \quad (61)$$

$$\text{AINV.K} = \text{TABLE}(\text{TIME.K}) \quad \text{Autonomous investment demand} \quad (62)$$

$$\text{VAINV.KL} = \text{AINV.K}/\text{PRIND.K} \quad \text{Volume of autonomous investment demand} \quad (63)$$

$$\text{ICAC.KL} = \text{DELAY}(\text{SSII.JK}) \quad \text{Induced capital acquisition} \quad (64)$$

$$\text{CDEP.KL} = (\text{CAP.K})(\text{ROD}) \quad \text{Capital depreciation} \quad (65)$$

$$\text{IINV.KL} = \text{MAX}\left(\frac{\text{DESCAP.K} - \text{CAP.K}}{\text{ADE}}, 0\right) \quad \text{Induced investment demand (volume)} \quad (66)$$

$$\text{DESCAP.K} = (\text{DVNOP.K})(\text{COR.K}) \quad \text{Desired capital} \quad (67)$$

$$\text{COR.K} = \text{TABLE}(\text{SRGNPC.K}) \quad \text{Capital output ratio} \quad (68)$$

Equation 62 allows the simulation of alternative strategies of government spending in relation to oil production and pricing policies (Equations 7, 9 and 11). The autonomous investment demand is not directly related to public savings. It is assumed that public spendings are actually financed by both the annual flows of public savings and the accumulated financial reserves so that, for a given year, government expenditures can be larger than corresponding savings. The quantification of Equation 62 defines major economic and development options. A low level of government spending, relative to the income flows, generates moderate industrial development and diversification and a large accumulation of financial assets. A high level of government spending privileges domestic accumulation and industrial diversification to the detriment of financial accumulation.

Figure 4.8: Assumed Changes in the Capital Output Ratio. Changes in USA's Capital Output Ratio

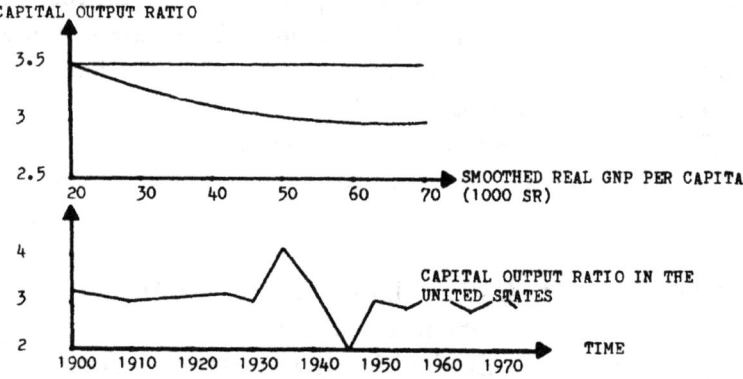

Table 4.3: Estimated Capital Output Ratios and Labour Output Ratios in the Non-Oil Sector

1954–1958	increment in the national capital stock	1,675 m SR
	increment in the national value added	735 m SR
	incremental capital output ratio	2.3
1963	capital invested in selected manufacturing industries	117.9 m SR
	value of gross output	62 m SR
	capital output ratio	1.9
1968/69	capital invested in PETROMIN projects	553.5 m SR
	total net output	148.7 m SR
	capital output ratio	3.72
1972	capital invested in private manufacturing sector	859 m SR
	net value added	499 m SR
	employment	36,012
	capital output ratio	1.72
	labour output ratio	0.127
Projection for 1980	capital invested in private manufacturing sector	8,101 m SR
	gross value added	2,606 m SR
	employment	70,200
	capital output ratio	3.11
	labour output ratio*	0.0474
Projects identified for the Second Development Plan (manufacturing)	capital invested	4,711 m SR
	gross value added	1,140 m SR
	employment	14,653
	capital output ratio	4.13
	labour output ratio*	0.023

* Hours worked per SR of value added. The labour output ratio is computed assuming an average of 1,760 man hours per year.

Sources: United Nations, Second Development Plan.

Factors of Production

In this case, however, the impact of domestic inflation can be substantially reinforced. As for the policy decisions regulating the oil sector, the implications of public spending policies are extremely important. A detailed analysis of these implications is provided in the second part of the book.

The capital output ratio (Equation 68) indicates the capital requirements of the production process and, together with the labour output ratios, measures the average efficiency of this process. The model allows the capital output ratio to vary (Figure 4.8) although several studies have shown, for various countries, a remarkable long-range stability of this ratio. In the United States, for example, the capital output ratio has remained close to 3 from 1900 to 1970.

Table 4.3 gives various estimations of both the capital output ratio and the labour output ratio in Saudi Arabia from 1954 to 1980.

The model considers an average capital output ratio of 3.5. This ratio is supposed either to remain constant or to moderately decrease as the real gross national product per capita increases.

The Financial Assets

The financial assets are not directly a factor of production but a reserve for future industrial investments or other domestic usages. The large monetary and financial reserves that Saudi Arabia is presently building up (Table 4.4) result from the kingdom's willingness to produce crude oil at a rate far higher than its development needs call for and its economy can absorb.

The level of financial assets is the result of the accumulation of the net annual surpluses generated by the economic system. These surpluses occur when the net resources generated by the economy are greater than the total expenditures of the various economic agents. In equation form, this is:

$$\text{FINAS.K} = \text{FINAS.J} + (\text{DT})(\text{NSUR.JK}) \quad \text{Financial assets} \quad (69)$$
$$\text{NSUR.KL} = \text{GNP.K} - (\text{SSC.JK} + \text{ACAC.JK} + \text{ICAC.JK})$$
$$(\text{PRIND.K}) \quad \text{Surplus} \quad (70)$$

The surplus (Equation 70) is either positive or negative. A positive surplus indicates that the economy is unable to recycle totally the flow of net income that it has generated. A negative surplus indicates that the economy needs additional resources to finance its domestic development. The model assumes that the financial assets are invested abroad and generate yearly returns. A negative surplus consequently

Table 4.4: Saudi Arabia's Financial Reserves

		International liquidity (millions of US $)		Sama's foreign assets (millions of SR)
	Gold	Foreign exchange	International reserves*	
1969	119	465	607	3,534
1970	119	520	662	4,021
1971	117	1,291	1,444	6,946
1972	117	2,347	2,500	11,992
1973	130	3,707	3,877	16,993
1974	132	13,424	14,285	73,147
1975	126	21,355	23,319	138,645

* Includes gold and foreign exchange.
Sources: Saudi Arabian Monetary Agency, IMF.

implies the repatriation of financial resources and decreasing returns.

Structural Analysis

The four substructures described in this chapter are represented in Figures 4.9, 4.10, 4.11 and 4.12. Figure 4.9 shows the four feedback loops controlling the population level, together with some of the loops that link the substructure to other substructures of the model. The four feedback loops that constitute the internal structure of the population sector describe the basic dynamics of population growth. There are two positive loops that, through the number of births, tend to increase the population level and two negative loops that, through the number of deaths, tend to decrease this level. These loops include two variables: the real GNP per capita and the wealth per capita through which the population sector is related to other sectors of the economy. As the population level also affects these sectors, there are additional loops which link several substructures of the model. The relationship shown in Figure 4.9 can be summarized as shown in the diagram on page 59.

The loop that links population, the non-oil sector and the national accounts tends to reduce the population level if a given increase in this level generates a higher increase in the gross national product.

Factors of Production

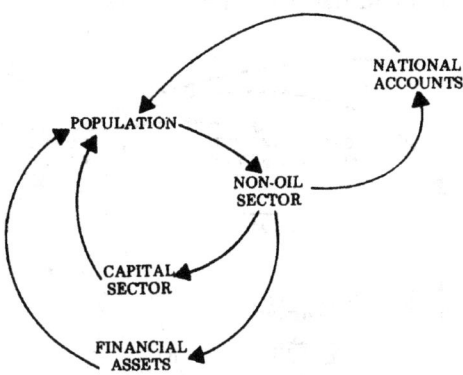

In this case, the GNP per capita increases which results in a decrease in the birth rate. This mechanism also depends upon the Saudi labour output ratio and involves the loop that links population, the non-oil sector and the capital sector. This loop is composed of several basic loops (Figure 4.9) and has a positive effect on the above system.

Population growth positively affects the labour force and leads to a larger volume of production which implies more capital accumulation, a decrease in the death rate and a more efficient labour force. These effects generate, by feedback, induced positive changes in the population level. However, an increase in population also induces negative effects that limit its growth. The actual behaviour of the population level results from the relative impact of each loop and cannot be anticipated by studying the internal structure of the population sector in isolation.

Figure 4.10 shows the loops that control the level of foreign labour force. The internal structure of the sector is composed of two loops of opposite polarity. The diagram also shows several additional loops that involve other substructures of the model. An increase in the level of foreign labour force generates two effects which induce opposite feedback responses. The positive effect results from the fact that an increase in the labour force reduces productive capital per worker which causes the foreign labour output ratio to increase and foreign labour demand to rise. The negative effect is the consequence of the fact that, as the foreign labour force grows, the gap between the production capacity from capital and the production capacity from labour is progressively filled which causes foreign labour demand to decrease. The most important factor that determines the level of the foreign labour force in the kingdom is, however, the process of capital accumulation. As long as the Saudi population does

Figure 4.9: Population and the Saudi Labour Force

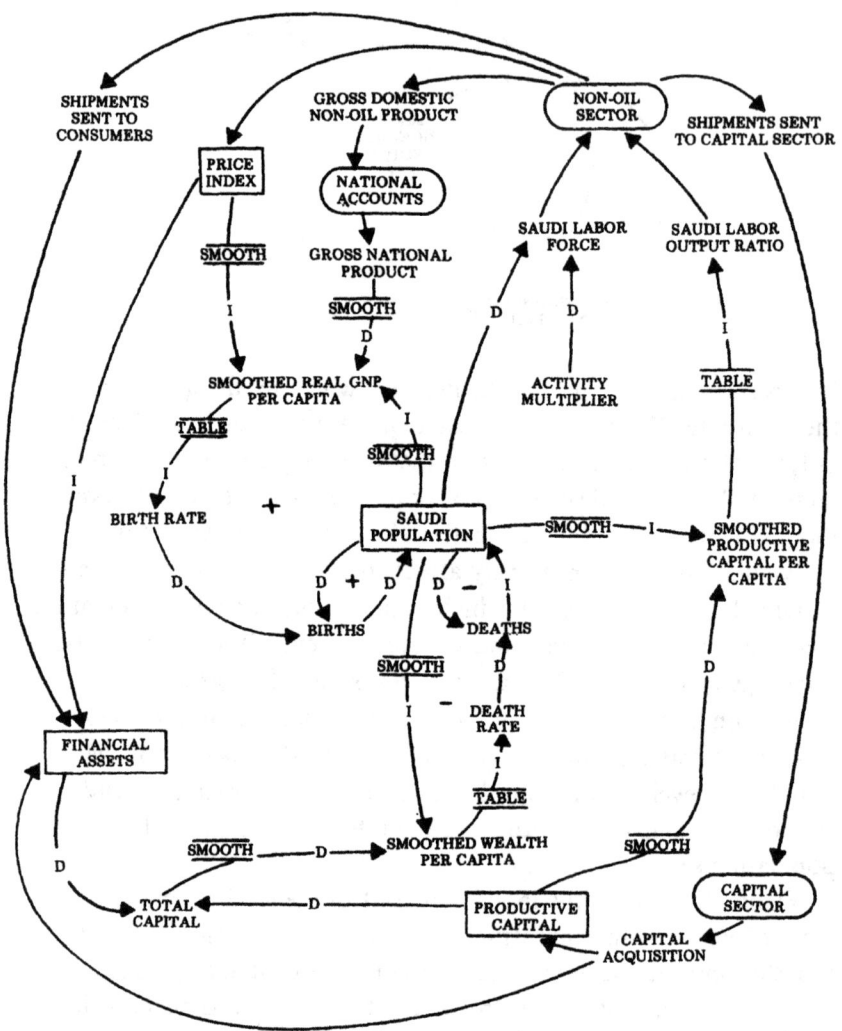

not provide the economy with the labour resources that are required to balance the production processes, i.e. to match the production capacity resulting from capital accumulation, foreign labour resources will be imported.

The capital sector is represented in Figure 4.11. The diagram shows the three loops which, through induced investment demand, link the capital sector to the non-oil sector. The process of capital

Factors of Production

Figure 4.10: Foreign Labour Force

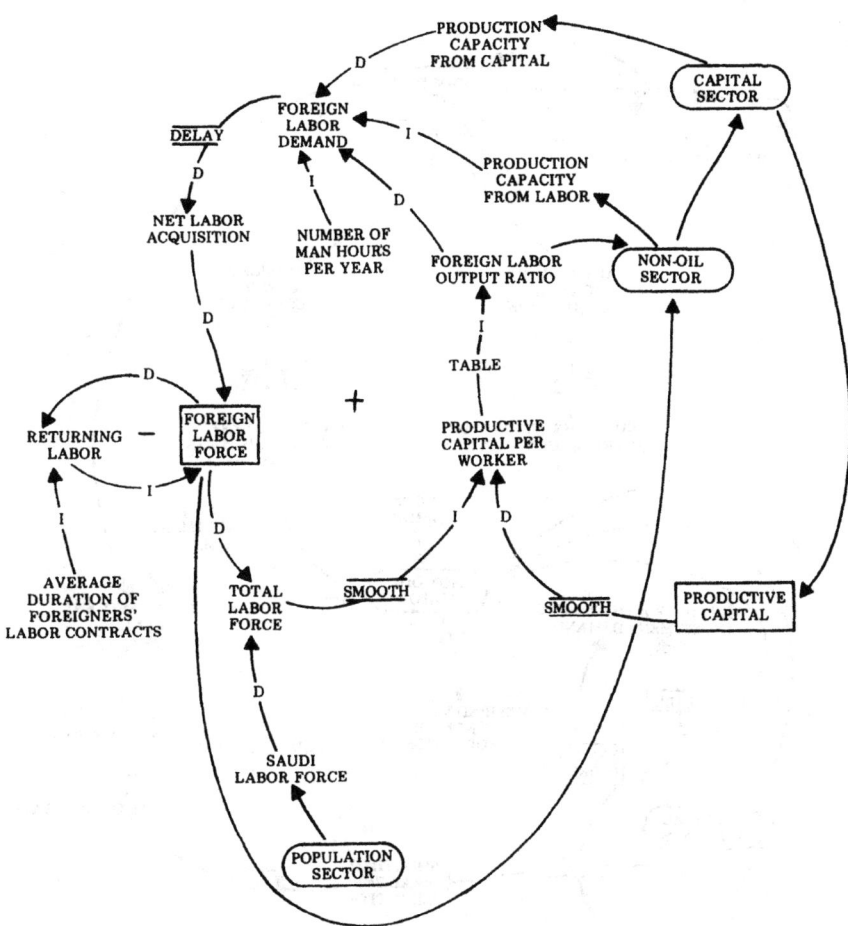

accumulation is activated by an exogenous policy, the autonomous investment demand, and by a mechanism of capital adjustment, the purpose of which is to match actual and desired capital. In addition, there is a negative loop on the productive capital level which describes the mechanism of capital depreciation. The loops shown in Figure 4.11 only constitute a partial representation of the dynamics of capital accumulation. There exist other loops which result from the fact that the capital sector affects and is affected by other substructures of the model. The capital-output ratio, for example, is affected by both

Figure 4.11: The Capital Sector

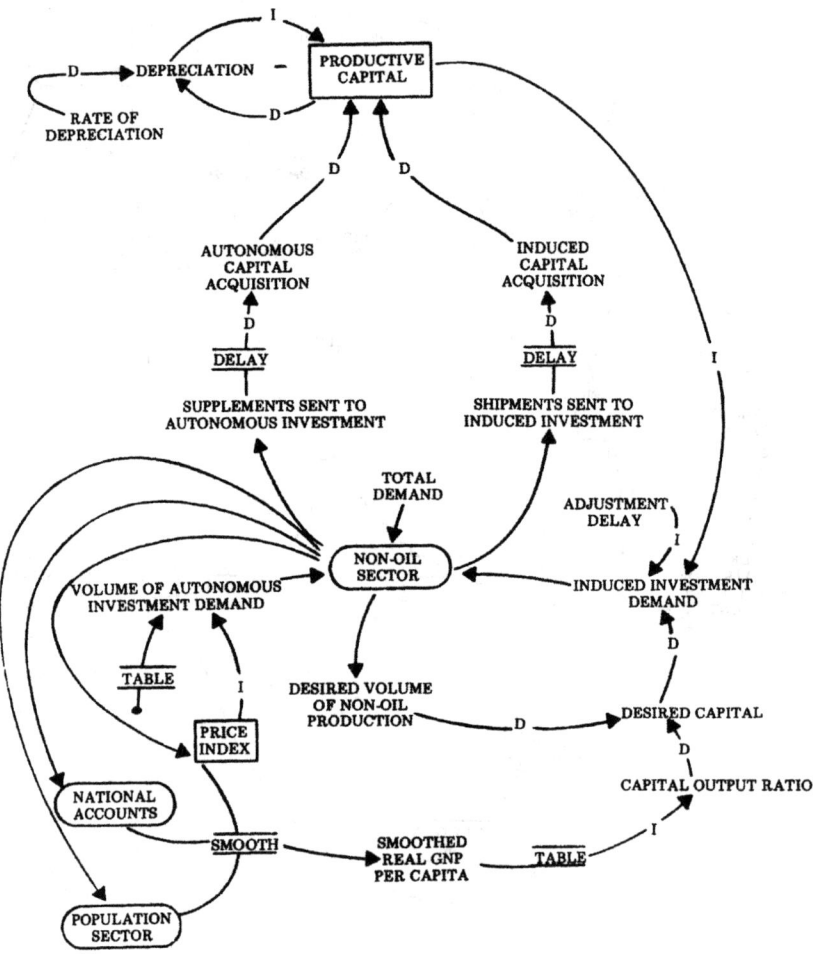

the national account substructure and the population sector which, themselves, are affected by the non-oil sector and the capital sector.

The financial assets are shown in Figure 4.12. The major loop of this substructure is positive. An increase in the level of financial assets generates increased returns and leads to an induced increase in the gross national product. A higher gross national product causing the net surplus to rise, the level of financial assets increases again.

As was mentioned previously, the actual behaviour of the economy results from the addition of all the effects that have been analyzed on

The Factors of Production

Figure 4.12: The Financial Assets

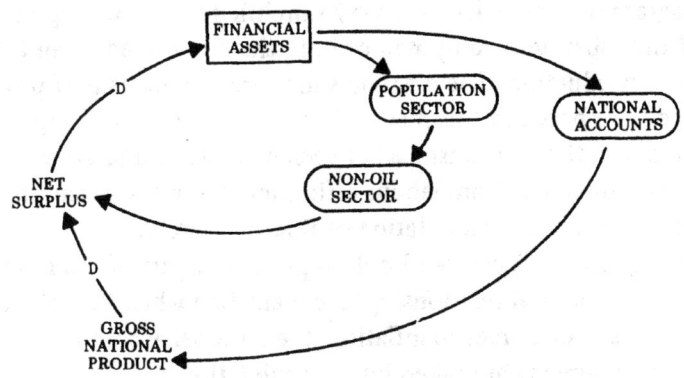

Figure 4.13: The Non-Oil Sector and the Factors of Production. Simplified Representation

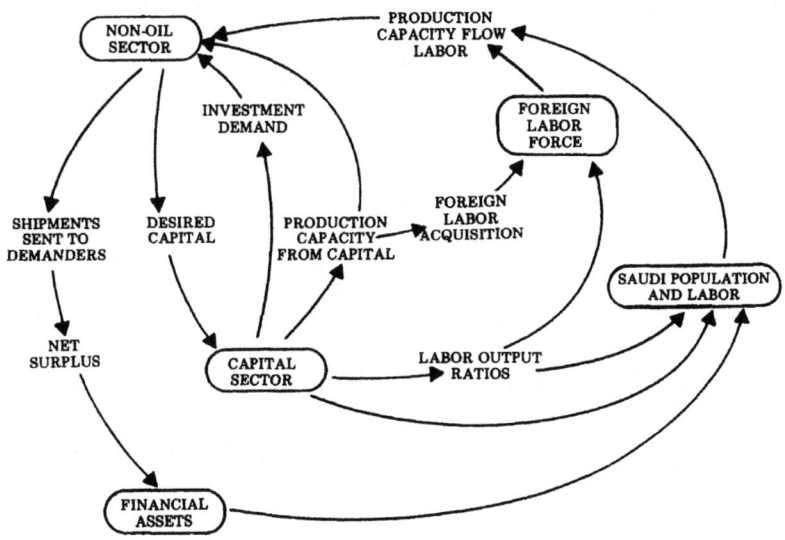

an individual basis and cannot be anticipated by studying any of these effects in isolation. It is therefore essential to understand the overall mechanism which results from the assemblage of the various substructures. However, assembling the substructures of the model leads to complex diagrams that become rapidly incomprehensible if they are not simplified. Figure 4.13 provides such a simplification. The diagram of Figure 4.13 is a very simplified structural representation of the subsystem composed of both the non-oil sector and the factors of production. The diagram shows the mechanism of production, the links between this mechanism and the process of capital accumulation, the relationships between capital accumulation, foreign labour acquisition, labour efficiency, the mechanism of production, and the accumulation of financial reserves.

The diagram of Figure 4.13 only represents a part of the model. Additional structural relationships are identified when the oil sector, the mechanism of domestic inflation, the national accounts and the balance of payments are taken into consideration.

5 THE MECHANISM OF DOMESTIC INFLATION

Inflation is presently one of the most serious domestic problems of the kingdom. According to United Nations' estimates, the increase in consumer prices was 4.4 per cent in 1971 and 1972, 16.5 per cent in 1973, 21.4 per cent in 1974 and 35.4 per cent in 1975. The changes in the consumer price index are given in Table 5.1. It is furthermore estimated that the 1976 rate of global inflation varied between 40 and 60 per cent.

Table 5.1: Changes in the Consumer Price Index

1969	1970	1971	1972	1973	1974	1975
99.8	100	104.5	109	127	154.2	207.6

1973				1974				1975				1976
I	II	III	IV	I	II	III	IV	I	II	III	IV	I
124	132.2	127.5	133.3	145.4	148.9	159.2	163.4	191.1	207.8	207.9	233.1	248.7

Source: IMF.

Global inflation results from various causes and affects most of the sectors of the economy. The Saudi Arabian economy is heavily dependent upon foreign trade and the Saudi imports constitute a considerable proportion of the total supply of the non-oil sector (Table 5.2). As a result, domestic inflation is significantly affected by rising import prices. The IMF export price index for developed countries indicated an additional increase of 24 per cent in 1974 compared with 22 per cent in 1973, 7.6 per cent in 1972 and 5 per cent in 1971.

A secondary inflationary effect results from potential discrepancies between the growth rate of salaries and wages and the growth rate of labour efficiency. If salaries and wages grow faster than productivity, the economy is spending money that it did not earn and the monetary surplus is absorbed through an increase in the level of prices.

A third cause of inflation is the occurence of a gap between total demand and total supply. The infusion into the economy of far more money than it can possibly absorb generates a dynamic process that

Table 5.2: Imports and Non-Oil Production

	Imports (millions of SR)	Non-oil production (millions of SR)	Import/non-oil production (%)
1968	4,392	7,764	57
1969	4,851	8,705	56
1970	4,990	9,293	54
1971	5,205	10,340	50
1972	6,303	11,325	56
1973	8,272	14,267	58
1974	13,192	21,245	62
1975	18,612	27,485	68
1976	37,000*	n.a.	n.a.

* Estimated.
Source: Saudi Arabian Monetary Agency.

leads the economic system to move from an initial inflationless equilibrium to another state of equilibrium which is achieved through an increase in the level of prices.

The structure of the mechanism of inflation, which is based upon these three effects — import effect, salary effect and demand effect — is shown in Figure 5.1.

The model assumes that the variations of the price index can be directly controlled and indirectly regulated through governmental consumption and investment policies. In addition, the government is assumed to entirely control the creation of money, that is, the banking system.

The diagram of Figure 5.1 shows that inflation affects each major component of the structure of the economic system except the oil sector. The price index is a very important variable that can deeply modify the process of economic growth in the non-oil sector and even, indirectly, the oil production policy. A high rate of inflation might lead to a significant reduction in government expenditures which would result in larger investments in financial assets, this increase in the level of financial assets affecting the production of crude oil through the absorption multiplier (Figure 2.2). The major consequence of a persistent inflation is to increase the cost of the development

The Mechanism of Domestic Inflation

Figure 5.1: The Strucutre of the Mechanism of Inflation

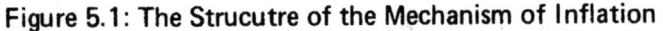

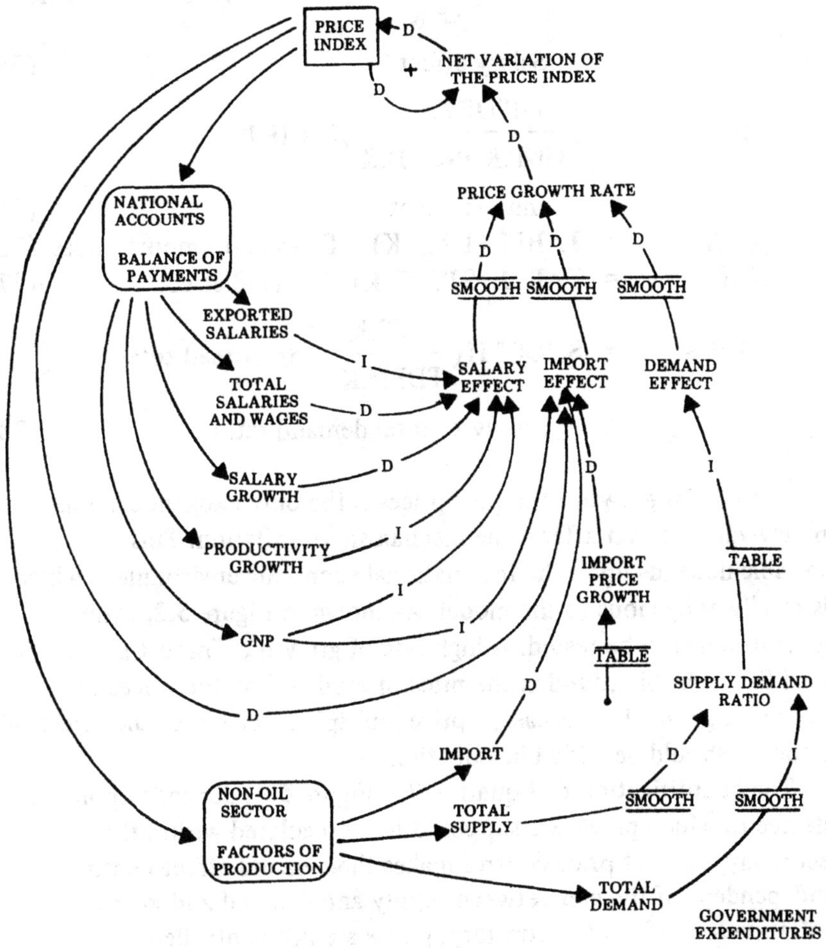

programme, that is, to make each barrel of exported crude oil less profitable in terms of domestic development.

In equation form, the mechanism of inflation is described as follows:

PRIND.K	= PRIND.J + (DT) (NPVAR.JK) Price index	(71) (71
NPVAR.KL	= (PRRG.K)(PRIND.K) Net price index variation	(72)
PRRG.K	= SMOOTH (SEF.K + IPEF.K + DEF.K) Price growth	(73)

68 *The Anatomy of the Saudi Arabian Economy*

$$\text{SEF.K} = \left(\frac{\text{SAL.K} - \text{EXSAL.K}}{\text{GNP.K}}\right)(\text{RGSA.K} - \text{RGOM.K})$$

Salary effect (74)

$$\text{IPEF.K} = \left(\frac{\text{IMPORT.K}}{\text{GNP.K}/\text{PRIND.K}}\right)(\text{RGIP.K})$$

Import effect (75)

RGIP.K = TABLE(TIME.K)   Growth of import prices (76)
DEF.K = TABLE(STSDR.K)   Demand effect (77)

$$\text{STSDR.K} = \text{SMOOTH}\left(\frac{\text{TSS.K}}{\text{TDEM.K}}\right) \text{ Smoothed total}$$

supply to total demand ratio (78)

The rate of growth of import prices is the only exogenous, non-policy variable that affects the mechanism of inflation. This variable depends upon the international economic environment which is totally exogenous to the model. As shown in Figure 5.2, various assumptions can be tested. A high rate of growth of import prices might lead Saudi Arabia to index the price of crude oil on the prices of imported goods. In this case, a price multiplier, related to the prices of imports, should be added in Equation 16.

The quantification of Equation 77 (Figure 5.3) depends upon the degree to which prices are supposed to be regulated within the economy. A strict price control makes the demand effect relatively independent of the gap between supply and demand and keeps inflation low. If, on the contrary, prices are not controlled, the

Figure 5.2: Growth of Import Prices. Possible Assumptions

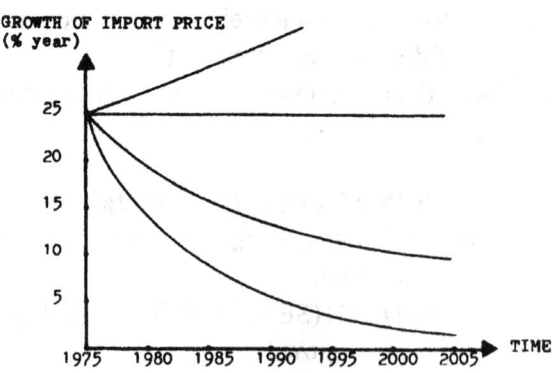

The Mechanism of Domestic Inflation

Figure 5.3: Demand Effect on Domestic Inflation

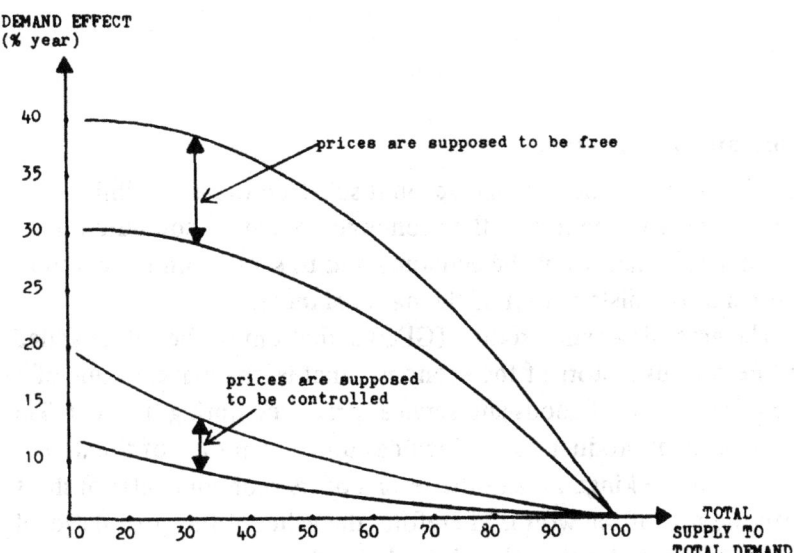

allocation of available supply to global demand is regulated by the market, that is, by the prices, and the demand effect is very sensitive to changes in the supply demand ratio.

The model is extremely sensitive to the structure of Equation 77, especially when it is assumed that prices are freely determined by the conditions of the market. For example, if the economic development of the kingdom requires annual public expenditures of, say, sixty billion riyals during ten years, the cost of this ten year develop-programme is, in an inflationless environment, six hundred billion riyals, that is, roughly, fourteen billion barrels of crude oil at the 1976 price. If now it is assumed that the conditions of the market are such that the average domestic inflation rate is 10 per cent a year, the actual development cost is

$$60 + 60(1.1) + 60(1.1)^2 + 60(1.1)^3 + ... + 60(1.1)^9$$

that is, 956 billion riyals or an increase of 59 per cent on the inflationless development cost. It goes without saying that the persistence in the long-range of the present domestic inflation rate would lead to massive development costs that the economy would simply not be able to support.

6 THE NATIONAL ACCOUNTS AND THE BALANCE OF PAYMENTS

The National Accounts

The functions of the national account substructure are to link the oil sector to the rest of the economic system, to compute the annual performances of the economy and to show both the composition and the distribution of the national income.

The gross domestic product (GDP) is the sum of the values added by the various sectors of the economy, that is, the market value of the total output of goods and services produced during the year. The gross national product (GNP) includes both the results of the domestic activity of the kingdom and the results of its economic relationships with the rest of the world. Therefore, the value of the gross national product is given by the following relationship:

$$GNP = GDP - \text{all payments abroad} + \text{all incomes from abroad}$$

Incomes from and payments abroad constitute the balance of payments. The gross national product is, in Saudi Arabia, the most revealing indicator of the kingdom's global economic activity because of the numerous inter-relations that link the Saudi Arabian economy to the rest of the world.

The national income is equivalent to the gross national product but focuses on the distributive aspects of the national output. The national income is composed of two elements: salaries and wages after payments abroad and profits after payments abroad. This income generates a national demand which is distributed into consumer demand and saving (Figure 6.1 and Table 6.1).

Both the composition and the distribution of the national income depend upon behavioural patterns. On the composition side, the model endogenously computes the wage rate and determines the global profit by difference. Salaries and wages are assumed to vary as a function of the changes in both the inflation rate and the output per man hour taken as an estimate of the average labour efficiency. The production of crude oil being a highly capital-intensive activity, the output per man hour is computed on the sole basis of the gross domestic non-oil product which is considered a better basis for the estimation of the average labour efficiency.

Thus, in 1975, the average annual output per man was:

$$\frac{27{,}485}{1.6} = 17{,}178 \text{ riyals}$$

which corresponds to an output per man hour of 9.6 riyals. If the 1975 output per man is taken as the initial average annual salary, the corresponding average monthly salary is 1,430 riyals. This assumption is consistent with a 1972 estimate stating that the average monthly salary in that year was 710 riyals and with an average rate of growth of salaries and wages slightly greater than twenty-five per cent a year during the period 1972–1975.

On the distribution side, the model only computes the consumer demand since the investment demands are not directly related to the annual saving flows. Consumer demand is supposed to be a variable proportion of the gross national product and is also affected by an exogenous multiplier taking into consideration government expenditures in consumption goods. The percentage of the national income allocated to consumption demand is derived from the propensity to consume which depends upon three multipliers: the inflation multiplier, the product availability multiplier and the wealth multiplier which are respectively related to the inflation rate, the ratio between shipments sent to consumers and consumer demand and the average wealth per capita.

In equation form, the national account substructure is described as follows:

$$\text{GDP.K} = \text{GDPOIL.K} + \text{GDPNOIL.K} \quad \text{Gross domestic product (value)} \quad (79)$$

$$\text{GDPNOIL.K} = (\text{VNOP.JK})(\text{PRIND.K}) \quad \text{Gross domestic non-oil product (value)} \quad (80)$$

$$\text{GNP.K} = \text{GDP.K} - \text{NPAB.K} \quad \text{Gross national product (value)} \quad (81)$$

$$\text{VCDEM.KL} = \text{CDEM.K}/\text{PRIND.K} \quad \text{Consumer demand (volume)} \quad (82)$$

$$\text{SCDEM.K} = \text{SMOOTH}(\text{VCDEM.JK}) \quad \text{Smoothed consumer demand (volume)} \quad (83)$$

$$\text{CDEM.K} = (\text{MPC.K})(\text{GOVMUL.K})(\text{DELAY}(\text{GNP.K})) \quad \text{Consumer demand (value)} \quad (84)$$

Table 6.1: The Saudi Arabian National Accounts (million SR current prices)

	1968	1969	1970	1971	1972	1973	1974	1975	1976*
GDP oil	6,893	7,270	8,106	12,581	16,932	26,284	79,720	121,232	n.a.
GDP non-oil	7,764	8,705	9,293	10,340	11,325	14,267	21,245	27,485	n.a.
TOTAL GDP	14,657	15,975	17,399	22,921	28,257	40,551	100,965	148,717	167,000
Net payments abroad	4,739	4,820	5,517	8,063	10,174	16,068	29,370	n.a.	n.a.
National income	9,918	11,155	11,882	14,858	18,083	24,483	71,595	n.a.	n.a.
Consumption expenditure	7,332	8,386	9,280	10,210	11,199	13,231	17,617	n.a.	n.a.
Capital formation	2,392	2,632	2,597	2,932	3,403	5,581	9,081	n.a.	n.a.
National expenditure	9,724	11,018	11,877	13,142	14,602	18,812	26,698	n.a.	n.a.
Net surplus	194	137	5	1,716	3,481	5,671	44,897	n.a.	n.a.
Imports	4,392	4,851	4,990	5,205	6,303	8,272	13,192	18,612	n.a.
Exports	8,589	9,086	10,302	15,189	19,862	30,012	87,459	97,380	n.a.
Balance of trade	4,197	4,235	5,312	9,984	13,559	21,740	74,267	78,768	n.a.

* Estimations

Sources: Saudi Arabian Monetary Agency, IMF, personal estimates.

The National Accounts and the Balance of Payments

Figure 6.1: Composition and Distribution of the Gross National Product

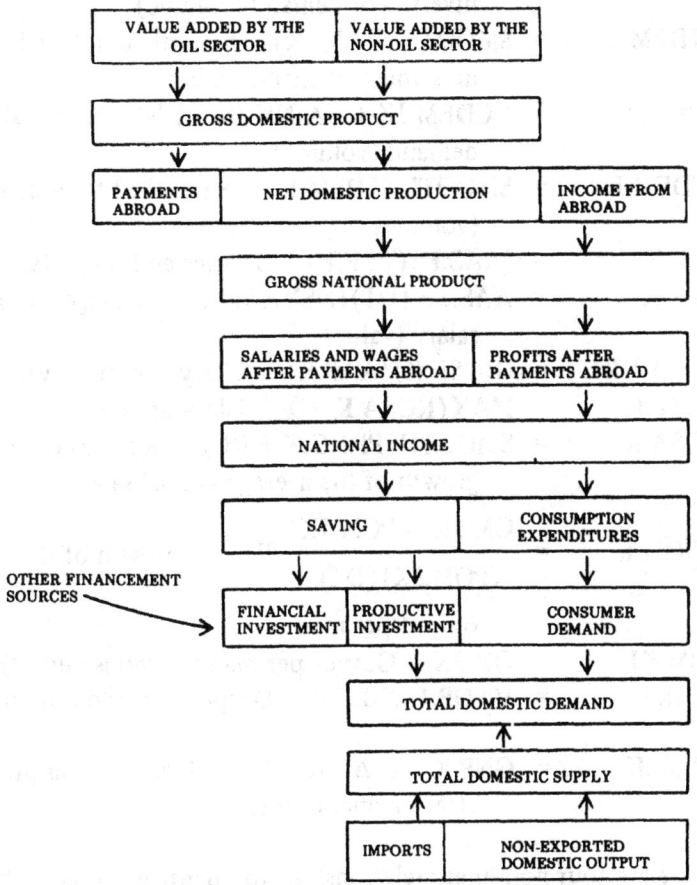

MPC.K	= (MPCN)(INMUL.K)(PAMU.K)(WMUL.K)	
	Propensity to consume	(85)
INMUL.K	= TABLE(PRRG.K) Inflation multiplier	(86)
PAMU.K	= TABLE(SSDR.K) Product availability	
	multiplier	(87)
SSDR.K	= SMOOTH(SSC.JK/VCDEM.JK) Supply	
	demand ratio (consumption)	(88)
WMUL.K	= TABLE(SWPC.K) Wealth multiplier	(89)
GOVMUL.K	= TABLE(TIME.K) Government multiplier	
	(consumption)	(90)
IDEM.K	= AINV.K + (IINV.K)(PRIND.K) Investment	

	demand (value)	(91)
SAIDEM.K	= SMOOTH(VAINV.JK) Smoothed autonomous investment demand (volume)	(92)
SIIDEM.K	= SMOOTH(IINV.JK) Smoothed induced investment demand (volume)	(93)
TDEM.K	= VCDEM.JK + VAINV.JK + IINV.JK Total demand (volume)	(94)
STDEM.K	= SMOOTH(TDEM.K) Smoothed total demand (volume)	(95)
SAL.K	= (AAS.K)(TLF.K) Salaries and wages (value)	(96)
AAS.K	= AAS.J + (DT)(NSVAR.JK) Average annual salary (value)	(97)
NSVAR.KL	= (RGSL.K)(AAS.K) Salary variation (value)	(98)
RGSL.K	= MAX(RGSA.K, 0) Salary growth	(99)
RGSA.K	= SMOOTH(PRRG.K + RGOM.K) Rate of growth of the average annual salary	(100)
RGOM.K	= $\dfrac{\text{OM.JK} - \text{POM.JK}}{(\text{POM.JK})(\text{DT})}$ Rate of growth of the output per man	(101)
POM.KL	= OM.JK Output per man (previous period)	(102)
OM.KL	= VNOP.JK/TLF.K Output per man (volume)	(103)
PROF.K	= GNP.K − (SAL.K − EXSAL.K) Total profits after payments abroad	(104)

There are four non-linear relationships to quantify. Three of them (Equations 86, 87 and 89) deal with consumers' behaviour and the fourth one (Equation 90) is a consumption demand regulator, i.e. an exogenous governmental policy.

The model assumes that, in a normal economic environment, there exists a fixed, normal proportion of the national income which is allocated to consumption expenditures (MPCN). This proportion, which is usually 65 per cent to 90 per cent of the national income, is however affected by changes in the economic environment such as inflation, the availability of consumer goods or the fact that consumers get richer. Inflation penalizes postponed expenditures by continously increasing the prices of goods and services. One may therefore expect that inflation is a significant incentive to increase the propensity to consume (Figure 6.2). This effect is part of the positive inflation-demand-inflation loop shown in Figure 5.1.

Figure 6.2: Effect of Inflation on the Normal Propensity to Consume

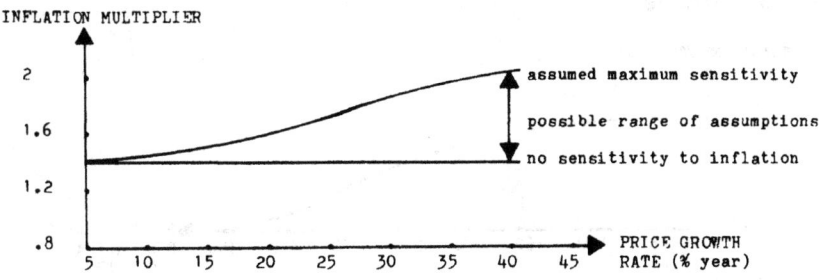

Figure 6.3: Effect of the Availability of Goods and Services on the Normal Propensity to Consume

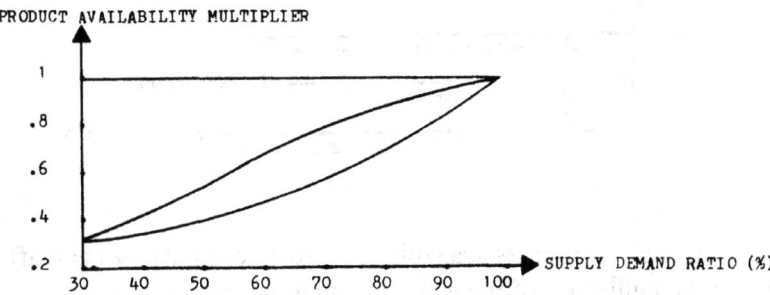

The availability of consumer goods, estimated in the model by the supply demand ratio concerning these goods, is an additional factor that positively affects the propensity to consume (Figure 6.3), especially when the economy is characterized by serious shortages, that is, when the difference between potential demand and actual product acquisition is large. The product availability multiplier is probably a major cause of the present very low propensity to consume in Saudi Arabia. Also significant is the income distribution.

At last, there exists a saturation effect on consumer demand: when customers get richer and when their consumption needs are satisfied, an increase in income is almost totally allocated to saving. The wealth multiplier is therefore a decreasing function of the wealth per capita (Figure 6.4).

The governmental regulation of consumption expenditures is a completely exogenous relationship for which several assumptions can be tested (Figure 6.5).

These four multipliers are important. They determine the annual

Figure 6.4: Effect of the Wealth Per Capita on the Propensity to Consume

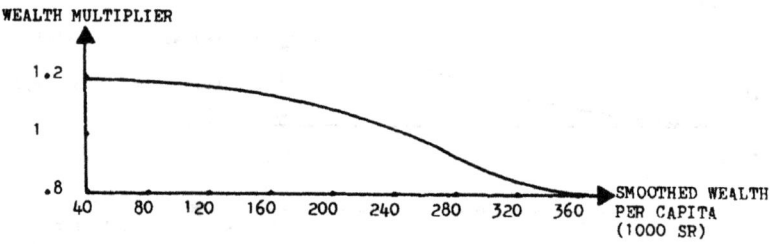

Figure 6.5: Assumed Governmental Consumption Policies

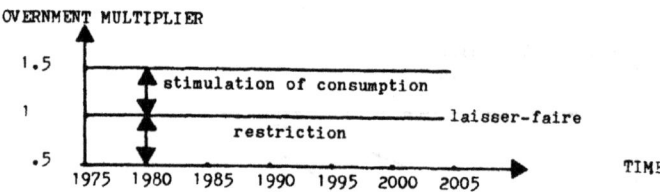

flow of financial resources available for investment purposes and affect the global equilibrium of the economy by either reinforcing or attenuating the impact of the demand flows on the economic system.

The Balance of Payments

The balance of payments is the account of the kingdom's economic relationships with the rest of the world. As the model relates imports and exports to the domestic activity of the kingdom, the balance of payments only considers financial and monetary transactions.
Figure 6.6 indicates the elements of the balance of payments that are taken into consideration by the model.

Exported salaries represent the remittances of expatriate workers

Figure 6.6: The Balance of Payments

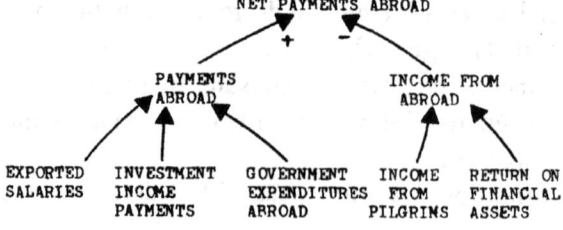

which have been valued at 1,138 million riyals in 1972, 1,932 in 1973, and 2,686 million riyals in 1974. The model assumes that the proportion of the salaries and wages paid to expatriate workers that is exported depends upon both an inflation multiplier and a product availability multiplier.

Investment income payments are presently the largest financial leakage. This net outflow of private investment income, mostly on account of Aramco, reached 41,026 million riyals in 1974, that is, 41 per cent of the 1974 GDP. Repatriation of profits by foreign companies is the major cause of the present negative difference between national income and gross domestic product. Full government ownership of the oil sector will significantly reduce this difference, but the development of new industries partly owned by foreigners will result again in the repatriation of profits. Also, payments abroad will increase as the number of foreign workers rises. The model assumes that investment income payments are a variable proportion of total profits. This proportion is related to the ratio of the Saudi labour force to the total labour force. This relationship is defined assuming a 100 per cent Saudi takeover of Aramco.

Government expenditures abroad represent the kingdom's inter-

Table 6.2: Major Elements of Saudi Arabia's Balance of Payments (m SR)

	Non-oil revenues	Income from pilgrimages	Investment income payments	Government expenditure abroad	Other payments
1964	126	239	1,733	315	436
1965	198	256	1,985	342	598
1966	234	266	2,727	365	643
1967	333	284	2,709	621	689
1968	360	324	3,118	1,215	752
1969	315	423	3,245	1,251	675
1970	405	459	4,018	1,206	747
1971	478	485	6,446	1,232	798
1972	655	653	8,496	1,240	1,138
1973	1,123	909	12,350	2,986	1,932
1974	4,790	1,665	41,026	7,465	2,686

Source: Saudi Arabian Monetary Agency.

78 The Anatomy of the Saudi Arabian Economy

national assistance. Foreign aid reached 7,465 million riyals in 1974, that is, 7.4 per cent of the 1974 GDP. This proportion is an exogenous policy variable in the model.

On the credit side, Saudi earnings on foreign investments are rising rapidly. The income from the kingdom's investments, handled by the Saudi Arabian Monetary Agency, reached 4.8 billion riyals in 1974. This income is expected to increase substantially in the near future. The income from pilgrimages is also a significant inflow. This income reached 1,665 million riyals in 1974. Both the rate of return on financial assets and the income from pilgrimages are exogenous variables in the model.

The major elements of the Saudi Arabian balance of payments are shown in Table 6.2.

The balance of payments is represented by the following equations:

NPAB.K	= EXSAL.K + IIP.K + GEA.K − PIL.K − ROFA.K Net payments abroad	(105)
EXSAL.K	= (EPS.K)(AAS.K)(FLF.K) Exported salaries	(106)
EPS.K	= (EPSN)(PAMUL.K)(INMU.K) Exported proportion of the expatriates' salaries	(107)
PAMUL.K	= TABLE(SSDR.K) Product availability multiplier	(108)
INMU.K	= TABLE(PRRG.K) Inflation multiplier	(109)
IIP.K	= DELAY((PFP.K)(PROF.K)) Investment income payments	(110)
PFP.K	= TABLE(SLF.K/TLF.K) Proportion of repatriated profits	(111)
GEA.K	= (PGH.K)(GDP.K) Government expenditures abroad	(112)
PGH.K	= TABLE(TIME.K) Proportion of government help	(113)
PIL.K	= (PILI)(1 + RGPIL.K)^t Pilgrimage income	(114)
RGPIL.K	= TABLE(TIME.K) Pilgrimage income growth	(115)
ROFA.K	= DELAY((ROR.K)(FINAS.K)) Return on financial assets	(116)
ROR.K	= TABLE(TIME.K) Rate of return	(117)

There are six non-linear relationships to quantify. Equation 107 is formulated as Equation 85: the model assumes that the normal

The National Accounts and the Balance of Payments 79

Figure 6.7: Effect of the Availability of Goods and Services on Exported Salaries

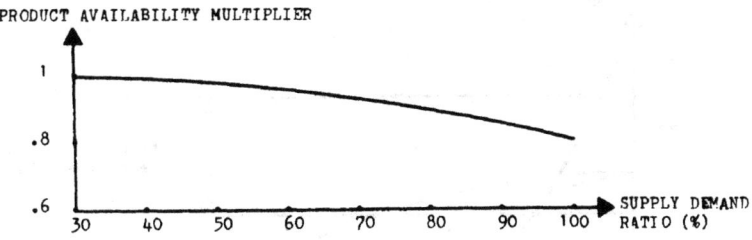

Figure 6.8: Effect of Inflation on Exported Salaries

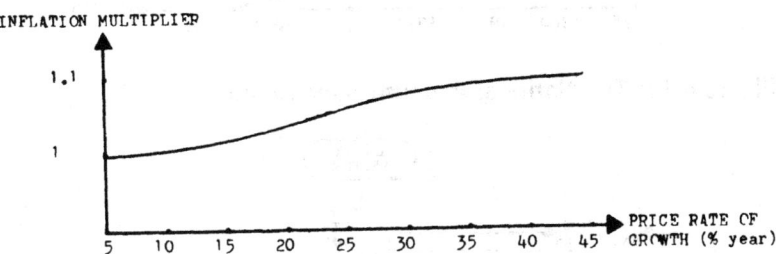

Figure 6.9: Proportion of Repatriated Profits

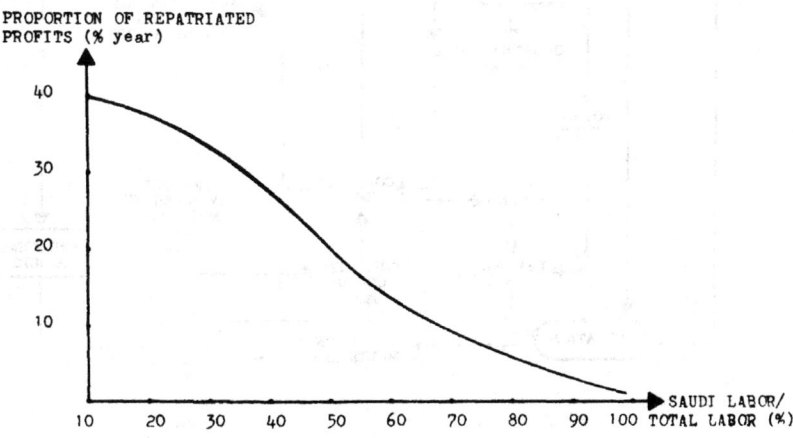

80 *The Anatomy of the Saudi Arabian Economy*

Figure 6.10: Exogenous Variables in the Balance of Payment Substructure

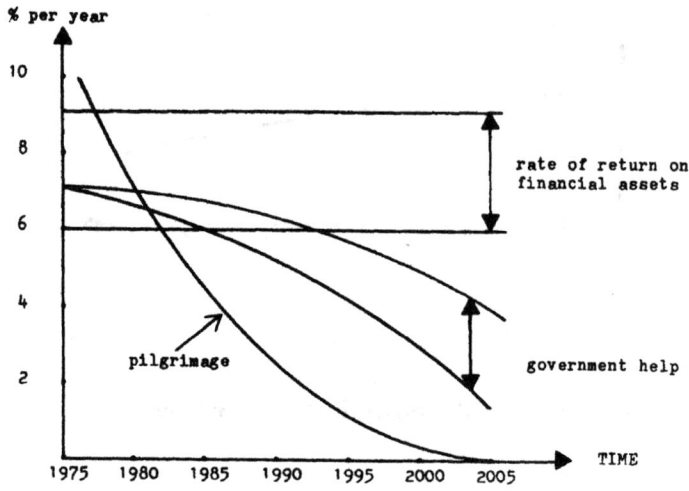

Figure 6.11: The National Account Substructure

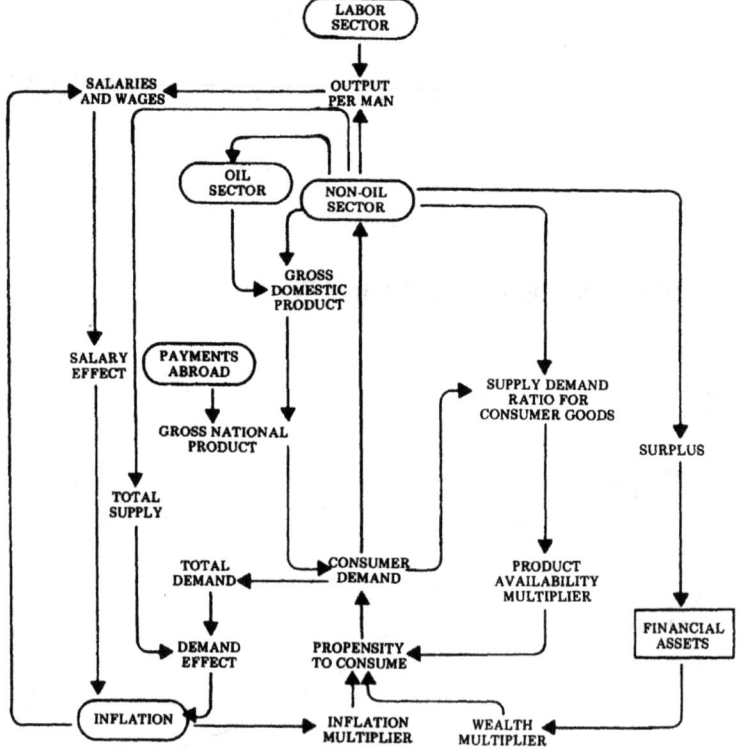

The National Accounts and the Balance of Payments

Figure 6.12: Payments Abroad

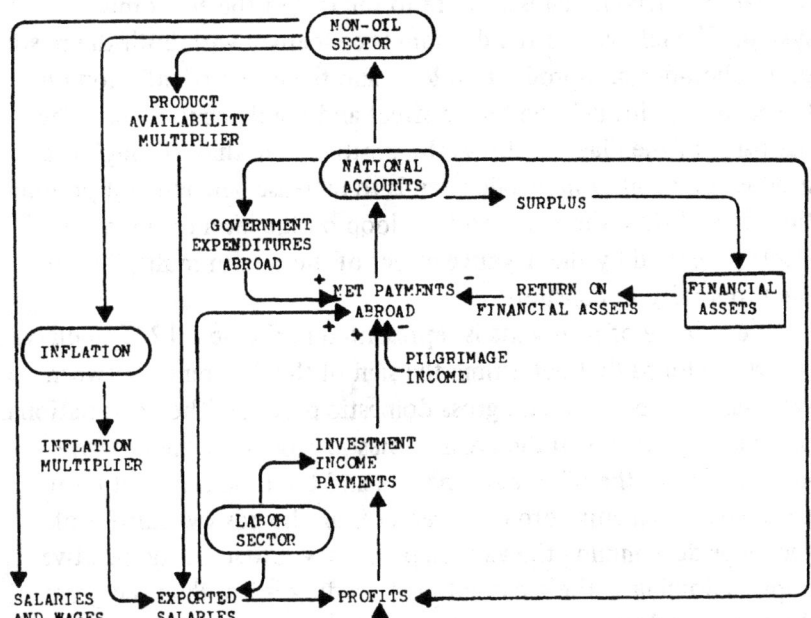

proportion of expatriates' salaries and wages which is exported — about sixty to sixty-five per cent of the total expatriates' salaries and wages — is affected by two multipliers. The product availability multiplier tends to reduce this proportion (Figure 6.7) whereas the inflation multiplier tends to increase it (Figure 6.8). The model however assumes that the effect of these multipliers is limited, the expatriate workers being supposed to minimize their expenditures in Saudi Arabia.

The proportion of repatriated profits (Equation 111) is supposed to decrease as the proportion of Saudi labour in the total labour force increases (Figure 6.9).

At last, the proportion of government help (Equation 113), the rate of growth of pilgrimage income (Equation 115), and the rate of return on financial assets (Equation 117) are totally exogenous. The first and the second variable are supposed to decrease through time and the third variable is assumed to be constant (Figure 6.10).

Structural Analysis

A simplified representation of the national account substructure is given in Figure 6.11. This diagram shows the major loops that link the national account substructure to the rest of the economic system. The left side of the diagram is concerned with both the positive production-demand-production loop and the effect of inflation on the economy through the salary effect and the demand effect. The right side of the diagram shows the positive loop that, through the product availability multiplier, tends to increase demand and production. In addition, there is a positive loop on the level of financial assets generated by the negative effect of the wealth multiplier on the propensity to consume.

The balance of payments is represented in Figure 6.12. The diagram shows the loops that determine the sign of the difference between gross national product and gross domestic product. The gross national product is greater than the gross domestic product if the negative impact of both the pilgrimage income and the financial asset loop on the net payments abroad is greater than the positive impact of the loops determining the various payments abroad. If the positive impacts dominate, the gross national product is less than the gross domestic product.

7 THE STRUCTURE OF THE ECONOMIC SYSTEM

The Model

The complete simulation model is a dynamic system of 117 equations including 12 levels, 29 numerical tables, 15 exogenous variables or coefficients, 7 policy variables, and 24 DELAY and SMOOTH functions. The equations are:

Reserves of Crude Oil

ORES.K   = ORES.J + (DT)(DISCO.JK − COP.JK)
DISCO.KL = (DIRAT.K)(ORES.K)
DIRAT.K   = TABLE(ACOP.K)
ACOP.K   = ACOP.J + (DT)(COP.JK)

Crude Oil Production

COP.KL   = COPEX.K + DOMUS.K

Production for Export

COPEX.K = (PRN.K)(ACMUL.K)(OPMUL.K)
PRN.K   = (TABLE(SRPR.K))(365)   (POLICY)
SRPR.K   = SMOOTH(ORES.K/COP.JK)
ACMUL.K = TABLE(SAOR.K)   (POLICY)
SAOR.K   = SMOOTH(FINAS.K/GNP.K)
OPMUL.K = TABLE(SP.K)   (POLICY)

Domestic Usage

DOMUS.K = (EOR.K)(VNOP.JK)
EOR.K   = TABLE(CAPWO.K)
CAPWO.K = SMOOTH(CAP.K/TLF.K)

Gross Domestic Oil Product

GDPOIL.K = (SP.K)(COPEX.K)(ERSR)

Price of Crude Oil

$$SP.K = SMOOTH\left(\frac{MWD}{DWDA}\right) - \frac{COPEX.K}{(DWDA)(1+RGWD)} \quad t)$$

RGWD.K = TABLE(SP.K)

Supply to Consumers

UFOC.K = UFOC.J + (DT)(VCDEM.JK − SSC.JK)
SSC.KL = UFOC.K/DFOC.K
DFOC.K = TABLE(STOCK.K/SCDEM.K)

Supply to Autonomous Investment

UFOAI.K = UFOAI.J + (DT)(VAINV.JK − SSAI.JK)
SSAI.KL = UFOAI.K/DFOAI.K
DFOAI.K = TABLE(STOCK.K/SAIDEM.K)

Supply to Induced Investment

UFOII.K = UFOII.J + (DT)(IINV.JK − SSII.JK)
SSII.KL = UFOII.K/DFOII.K
DFOII.K = TABLE(STOCK.K/SIIDEM.K)

Inventory

STOCK.K = STOCK.J + (DT)(VNOP.JK + IMPORT.JK − SSC.JK − SSAI.JK − SSII.JK)

Non-Oil Production

VNOP.KL = MIN(PCAP.K, PCLAB.K)
PCAP.K = CAP.K/COR.K
PCLAB.K = PCSL.K + PCFL.K
PCSL.K = (SLF.K)(NHW)/SLOR.K
PCFL.K = (FLF.K)(NHW)/FLOR.K

Imports

IMPORT.KL = DELAY(DESIMP.K)
DESIMP.K = (DVNOP.K − VNOP.JK)/AD

Desired Non-Oil Production

DVNOP.K = STDEM.K + (DSTOCK.K − STOCK.K)/ADD

Desired Inventory

DSTOCK.K = (STM.K)(STSS.K)

The Structure of the Economic System

STM.K = TABLE(SSG.K)
SSG.K = SMOOTH(SG.K)
SG.K = (TSS.K − TSS.J)/(TSS.J)(DT)
TSS.K = SSC.JK + SSAI.JK + SSII.JK
STSS.K = SMOOTH(TSS.K)

Population

POP.K = POP.J + (DT)(NB.JK − ND.JK)
NB.KL = (BR.K)(POP.K)
BR.K = TABLE(SRGNPC.K)
SRGNPC.K = SMOOTH((GNP.K/PRIND.K)/POP.K)
ND.KL = (DR.K)(POP.K)
DR.K = TABLE(SWPC.K)
SWPC.K = SMOOTH(TCAP.K/POP.K)
TCAP.K = CAP.K + (FINAS.K/PRIND.K)

Saudi Labour Force

SLF.K = (AM.K)(POP.K)
AM.K = TABLE(TIME.K)   (POLICY)
SLOR.K = TABLE(SCAPCA.K)
SCAPCA.K = SMOOTH(CAP.K/POP.K)

Foreign Labour Force

FLF.K = FLF.J + (DT)(NLA.JK − RLAB.JK)
NLA.KL = DELAY(FLDE.K)
FLDE.K = (PCAP.K − PCLAB.K)(FLOR.K)/NHW
FLOR.K = TABLE(CAPWO.K)
RLAB.KL = FLF.K/ADFC
TLF.K = SLF.K + FLF.K

Productive Capital

CAP.K = CAP.J + (DT)(ACAC.JK + ICAC.JK − CDEP.JK)
ACAC.KL = DELAY(SSAI.JK)
AINV.K = TABLE(TIME.K)   (POLICY)
VAINV.KL = AINV.K/PRIND.K
ICAC.KL = DELAY(SSII.JK)
CDEP.KL = (CAP.K)(ROD)

$$\text{IINV.KL} = \text{MAX}\left(\frac{\text{DESCAP.K} - \text{CAP.K}}{\text{ADE}}, 0\right)$$

DESCAP.K = (DVNOP.K)(COR.K)

COR.K = TABLE(SRGNPC.K)

Financial Assets

FINAS.K = FINAS.J + (DT)(NSUR.JK)
NSUR.KL = GNP.K − (SSC.JK + ACAC.JK + ICAC.JK)
(PRIND.K)

Inflation

PRIND.K = PRIND.J + (DT)(NPVAR.JK)
NPVAR.KL = (PRRG.K)(PRIND.K)
PRRG.K = SMOOTH(SEF.K + IPEF.K + DEF.K)

$$SEF.K = \left(\frac{SAL.K - EXSAL.K}{GNP.K}\right)(RGSA.K - RGOM.K)$$

$$IPEF.K = \left(\frac{IMPORT.JK}{GNP.K/PRIND.K}\right)(RGIP.K)$$

RGIP.K = TABLE(TIME.K)
DEF.K = TABLE(STSDR.K)
STSDR.K = SMOOTH(TSS.K/TDEM.K)

Gross Domestic Product

GDP.K = GDPOIL.K + GDPNOIL.K
GDPNOIL.K = (VNOP.JK)(PRIND.K)

Gross National Product

GNP.K = GDP.K − NPAB.K

Consumer Demand

VCDEM.KL = CDEM.K/PRIND.K
SCDEM.K = SMOOTH(VCDEM.JK)
CDEM.K = (MPC.K)(GOVMUL.K)(DELAY(GNP.K))
MPC.K = (MPCN)(INMUL.K)(PAMU.K)(WMUL.K)
INMUL.K = TABLE(PRRG.K)
PAMU.K = TABLE(SSDR.K)
SSDR.K = SMOOTH(SSC.JK/VCDEM.JK)
WMUL.K = TABLE(SWPC.K)
GOVMUL.K = TABLE(TIME.K) (POLICY)

Investment Demand

IDEM.K = AINV.K + (IINV.K)(PRIND.K)

The Structure of the Economic System

SAIDEM.K = SMOOTH(VAINV.JK)
SIIDEM.K = SMOOTH(IINV.JK)

Total Demand

TDEM.K = VCDEM.JK + VAINV.JK + IINV.JK
STDEM.K = SMOOTH(TDEM.K)

Salaries and Wages

SAL.K = (AAS.K)(TLF.K)
AAS.K = AAS.J + (DT)(NSVAR.JK)
NSVAR.KL = (RGSL.K)(AAS.K)
RGSL.K = MAX(RGSA.K, O)
RGSA.K = SMOOTH(PRRG.K + RGOM.K)
RGOM.K = (OM.JK − POM.JK) / (POM.JK)(DT)
POM.KL = OM.JK
OM.KL = VNOP.JK/TLF.K

Profits

PROF.K = GNP.K − (SAL.K − EXSAL.K)

Payments Abroad

NPAB.K = EXSAL.K + IIP.K + GEA.K − PIL.K − ROFA.K

Exported Salaries

EXSAL.K = (EPS.K)(AAS.K)(FLF.K)
EPS.K = (EPSN)(PAMUL.K)(INMU.K)
PAMUL.K = TABLE(SSDR.K)
INMU.K = TABLE(PRRG.K)

Investment Income Payments

IIP.K = DELAY((PFP.K)(PROF.K))
PFP.K = TABLE(SLF.K/TLF.K)

Government Expenditures Abroad

GEA.K = (PGH.K)(GDP.K)
PGH.K = TABLE(TIME.K)   (POLICY)

Pilgrimages

PIL.K = $(PILI)(1 + RGPIL.K)^t$
RGPIL.K = TABLE(TIME.K)

Return on Financial Assets

ROFA.K   = DELAY((ROR.K)(FINAS.K))
ROR.K   = TABLE(TIME.K)

The 117 equations of the model constitute a set of logical assumptions about the structure of the Saudi Arabian economy. It is assumed, but it cannot be strictly verified, that the Saudi Arabian economy is correctly described by the model. These 117 equations are distributed in two categories: the structural assumptions and the policies. The difference is that, although any assumption can be modified, the structural assumptions, which define the economic and social environment, are more permanent than the policies, the purpose of which is to modify the environment in order to achieve predefined goals. Thus, a typical set of simulation experiments is organized as follows:

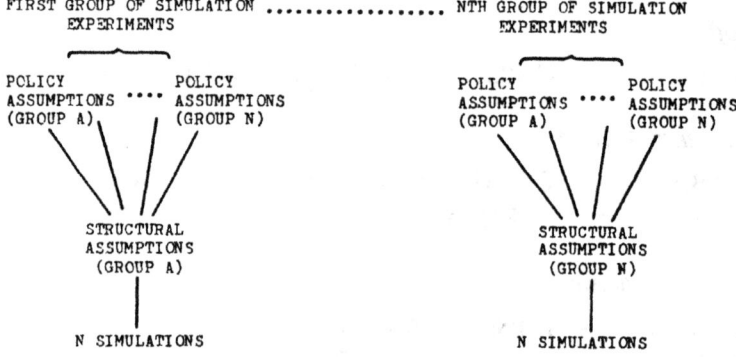

The model includes seven policy variables. Government policies are tested through changes in the seven TABLE functions that quantify these policies (Figure 7.1). In addition, there are potential policy variables that are not presently implemented but could be set up in the future, for example, fiscal policy, price control, limits on imported labour, exchange control (limits on repatriated salaries and profits), indexation of crude oil production on domestic inflation, etc. These additional policy variables can be introduced in the simulation programme together with their induced feedback effects.

Among the structural assumptions, there are fifteen exogenous variables. The initial values of the levels, of several non-level variables and the constants of the delays, which define the velocity of the response of these delays to given inputs, are also exogenous. Table 7.1

The Structure of the Economic System

Figure 7.1: Government Policies in the Model

GOVERNMENT POLICIES	SECTOR	VARIABLE NAME	TABLE NAME
Normal extraction rate	oil	PRN	OILTAB
Absorption multiplier	oil	ACMUL	TACMUL
Price multiplier	oil	OPMUL	TOPMUL
Activity multiplier	labor	AM	TAM
Autonomous investment	capital	AINV	TAINV
Government multiplier	nat. acc.	GOVMUL	GOTAB
Proportion of government help	balance of payments	PGH	PGHTAB

↓

MODEL
(SET OF STRUCTURAL ASSUMPTIONS)

↓

(RESULTS)

lists the fifteen non-policy, exogenous variables and Table 7.2 the constants of the delays of the model.

As a very large number of simulation experiments can be conducted, the model might be regarded as an over-flexible instrument that generates too many different sets of results to be really useful to decision makers.

However, similar features appear in simulation experiments resulting from different policy assumptions. If these simulation experiments are diverse enough to deal with the major development strategies that can be implemented, each feature that appears in most or all simulation experiments can be considered characteristic of the system's future and should be regarded an inevitable consequence of any policy decision.

Table 7.1: The Exogenous Variables of the Model

Variable name	Symbol	Type	Table name	Sector
Rate of exchange of the Riyal	ERSR	CONSTANT	—	Oil
Maximum world oil demand to Saudi Arabia	MWD	CONSTANT	—	Oil
Decrease in world demand for oil per additional US $ in price	DWDA	CONSTANT	—	Oil
Number of man hours per year	NHW	CONSTANT	—	Labour
Adjustment delay for desired import	AD	CONSTANT	—	Non-oil
Adjustment delay for desired volume of non-oil production	ADD	CONSTANT	—	Non-oil
Average duration of foreigners' labour contracts	ADFC	CONSTANT	—	Labour
Rate of capital depreciation	ROD	CONSTANT	—	Capital
Adjustment delay for induced investment	ADE	CONSTANT	—	Capital
Normal propensity to consume	MPCN	CONSTANT	—	National account
Normal exported proportion of expatriates' salaries	EPSN	CONSTANT	—	Balance of payments
Initial pilgrimage income	PILI	CONSTANT	—	Balance of payments
Rate of growth of import prices	RGIP	TABLE	TRGIP	Inflation
Rate of growth of pilgrimage income	RGPIL	TABLE	TRGPIL	Balance of payments
Rate of return on financial assets	ROR	TABLE	RORTAB	Balance of payments

The Structure of the Economic System

Table 7.2: The Constants of the Delays

Delayed variable	Delay type	Constant name	Sector
Reserve production ratio	SMOOTH	DSR	Oil
Financial asset to GNP ratio	SMOOTH	DSRA	Oil
Productive capital per worker	SMOOTH	DSRR	Oil labour
Price of crude oil	SMOOTH	DSP	Oil
Imports	DELAY	IDEL	Non-oil
Shipment growth	SMOOTH	DSSG	Non-oil
Total shipments sent	SMOOTH	DSTS	Non-oil
Real GNP per capita	SMOOTH	DSGNP	Population
Wealth per capita	SMOOTH	DSWPC	Population
Productive capital per capita	SMOOTH	DSCPC	Labour
Net labour acquisition	DELAY	LCD	Labour
Autonomous capital acquisition	DELAY	ACAD	Capital
Induced capital acquisition	DELAY	ICAD	Capital
Price rate of growth	SMOOTH	DSPV	Inflation
Total supply to total demand ratio	SMOOTH	DSRAT	Inflation
Consumer demand	SMOOTH	DSCD	National account
Consumer demand	DELAY	DIC	National account
Supply demand ratio for consumer goods	SMOOTH	DSRT	National account
Autonomous investment demand	SMOOTH	DSAID	National account
Induced investment demand	SMOOTH	DSIID	National account
Total demand	SMOOTH	DSDE	National account
Rate of growth of salaries and wages	SMOOTH	DSGSA	National account
Investment income payments	DELAY	DEP	Balance of payments
Return on financial assets	DELAY	RFAD	Balance of payments

Structural Analysis of the Economy

The dynamic structure of the economy is constituted by the connection of all previously analyzed substructures. The simplified diagram of Figure 1.1 shows the major features of the Saudi Arabian economy. Although simplified and very aggregated, this diagram includes the most important loops that determine the global behaviour of the economic system and shows how the implementation or the modification of

92 *The Anatomy of the Saudi Arabian Economy*

a given policy decision, or of several of them, affects this behaviour. The loops shown in Figure 1.1 can be distributed in five categories: the loops dealing with the process of industrialization, the loops concerned with the accumulation of financial assets, the loops generated by the mechanism of domestic inflation, the loops that link the oil sector to the rest of the economic system and the loops that interrelate industrialization and accumulation of financial assets. Each category of loops is, or could be, controlled by one or several policy decisions. Therefore, the behaviour of the economic system is closely dependent upon the decision to implement or not to implement a given policy as well as the strength of each policy decision. There is, however, a hierarchy of policy decisions: some are extremely important to the behaviour of the economy, some have limited effects.

As shown in the diagram below, the loops concerned with the process of industrialization are activated by the policy decision allocating financial resources to capital accumulation:

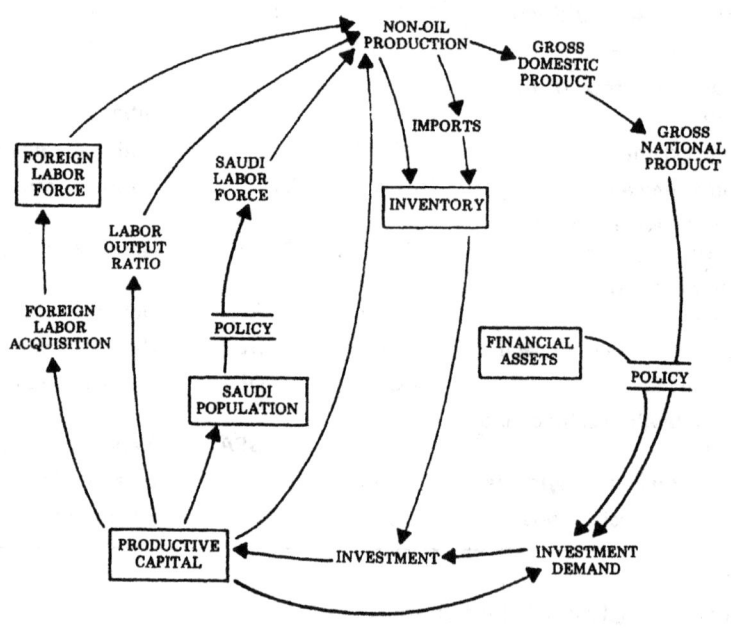

The exogenous investment policy is actually financed by two sources: the savings flows non affected to financial reserves and the financial reserves themselves. The saving flows affected to financial

The Structure of the Economic System

reserves, that is, the surplus, generate the financial asset loop:

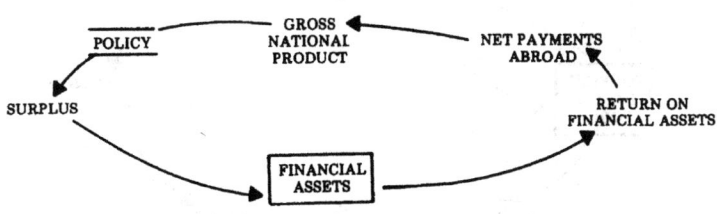

Therefore, the policy decision that distributes the income flows among capital accumulation and financial reserves is the policy decision that decides whether Saudi Arabia's economy will be based upon banking or upon industrialization. One of the major problems generated by industrialization programmes is inflation. A large demand taking place within an economy, the absorption capacity of which is limited, creates bottlenecks and shortages that the market mechanism compensates for through an increase in the level of prices:

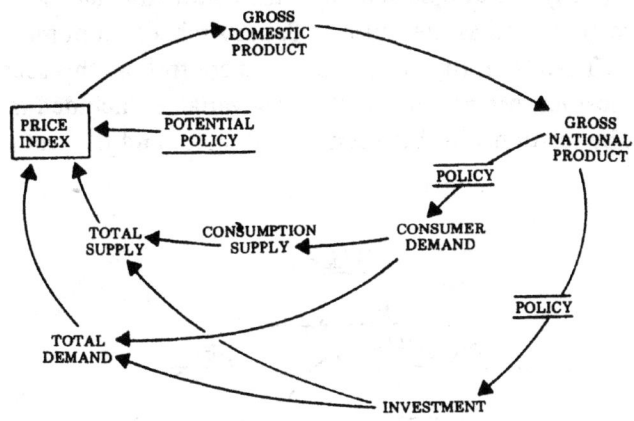

If demand is much larger than supply, the level of prices rises and the cost of the development programme is increased. The level of prices is indirectly regulated by the policy decisions controlling the government expenditures, which presently constitute a very significant proportion of total demand, and may be directly regulated by a price control policy (Figure 5.3).

The cost of the development programme is also affected by the repatriation of salaries and profits:

94 *The Anatomy of the Saudi Arabian Economy*

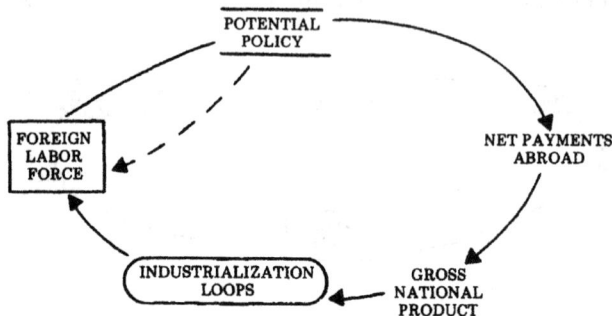

This variable may generate in the future large leakages (through the balance of payments) that might lead the government to control the repatriation of salaries and profits. However, such a policy might generate negative feedback effects on the acquisition of foreign labour.

The present driving force of the economy is the oil sector. This sector provides the economy with over-abundant sources of financing and is presently the unique source of the Saudi Arabian economic development as well as the cause of Saudi Arabia's economic problems. Therefore, the policy decisions controlling this sector are the most important among all policy variables included in the model. The relationships between the oil sector and the rest of the

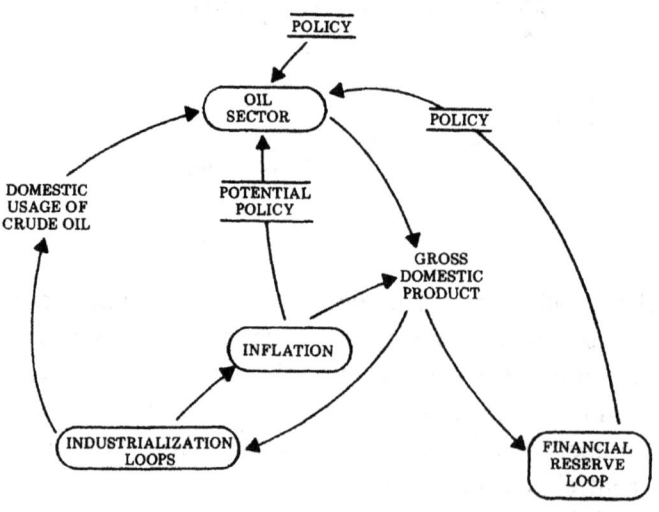

The Structure of the Economic System

economic system are, however, not clear. At present, the management of the oil sector seems totally independent of the domestic economic conditions. As shown in the above diagram, this situation might change in the future. In any case, the analysis of this problem requires a deeper approach that goes beyond the purpose of this book.

The Simulation Process

Simulation experiments with the model must be precisely organized and prepared. Tables 7.3 to 7.9 group in homogeneous categories the assumed numerical values of all constants and tables of the model. If not otherwise specified later in this book, these numerical values refer to all simulation experiments analyzed in the second part of the book. Table 7.3 gives the initial value of the twelve levels of the model together with the source of the data or the estimation procedure. Table 7.4 deals with the initial value of the non-level variables of the model that must be initialized. Tables 7.5, 7.6 and 7.7 indicate the numerical values of the structural assumptions of the model in the following order: exogenous constants, exogenous tables and endogenous tables. Table 7.8 gives the numerical value of the constants of the delays and Table 7.9 deals with the policy variables of the model.

Both the unit and the time dimension of each variable of the model has to be precisely defined (see Appendix 2). The reference time period of the model being the year, each variable that has a time dimension is defined in riyals, barrels, per cent, men, etc. per year. Similarly, each time constant is defined in years. The variables that do not have a time dimension are defined in riyals, barrels, per cent, men, etc. The choice of the size of the time interval DT depends upon the required numerical accuracy. In any case, DT should be smaller than or equal to half the velocity of the shortest delay.

Interpretation of the Results of the Model

The nature of the results supplied by a model is closely dependent upon the model type. The principles of this model methodology, system dynamics, are simple. The analyzed socio-economic system is described and quantified through a set of variables. The inter-relations that link these variables represent the physical structure of the system as well as the social, behavioural and political relationships constituting the information structure of the system, that is, the decisions and behaviours which determine the management of the physical structure of the system. The global structure of the system is composed of inter-connected feedback loops. Some

Table 7.3: Initial Value of the Levels

Name of the level	Assumed initial value	Unit	Source or estimation procedure
Reserves of crude oil	111,200	million bbl	Aramco (1975)
Cumulative production of crude oil	25,677	million bbl	OPEC (1975)
Inventory	22,230	million SR	note 1
Unfilled orders (consumers)	52,650	million SR	note 1
Unfilled orders (aut. inv.)	20,350	million SR	note 1
Unfilled orders (ind. inv.)	20,350	million SR	note 1
Productive capital	115,437	million SR	note 2
Average annual salary	17,178	thousand SR	previously explained
Saudi population	4,946	thousand	note 3
Foreign labour force	314	thousand	Second Development Plan (1976)
Financial assets	138,645	million SR	IMF (1975)
Price index	1	dimensionless	constant 1975 prices

1. It is assumed that the shipments sent to the consumers were 23.4 billion riyals in 1975, that is, a 33 per cent growth rate from 1974 to 1975 (similar to the 1973/74 growth rate). It is also assumed that the shipments sent to investors were 14.8 billion riyals in 1975, that is, a 63 per cent growth rate from 1974 to 1975 (similar to the 1973/74 growth rate). Total shipments sent being 37.2 billion riyals and the inventory multiplier being assumed to be 0.6 (about seven months), desired inventory is: (37.2) (0.6) = 22,320 million riyals. The initial inventory is assumed to be equal to the initial desired inventory. Assuming that, in 1975, supply matched demand and that investment demand was equally distributed among autonomous and induced demand, the inventory to demand ratios were 22,320/23,400 = 0.95 for consumption demand, and 22,320/7,400 = 3 for both autonomous and induced investment demands. The corresponding delays filling orders are given by the relationships shown in Figures 3.2 and 3.3, and the initial unfilled orders are computed as follows: unfilled orders = (shipments sent) (delay filling orders).
2. Assuming a 3.5 capital output ratio in the non-oil sector and a 20 per cent over-capacity.
3. Assuming that the Saudi labour force (1,286,000 according to the Second Development Plan) constitutes 26 per cent of total population.

of these loops generate growth processes whereas some other feedback loops act as regulators. The behaviour of the system results from the combined influence of both the positive and the negative loops and is determined by the dominant loops.

Table 7.4: Initial Value of the Non-Level Variables

Variable name	Assumed initial value	Unit	Source
Price of crude oil	12.4	US $/bbl	Chapter 2
Crude oil production for export	3,200	million bbl	Chapter 2
Volume of non-oil production	27,485	million SR	Second Development Plan
Desired volume of non-oil production	50,000	million SR	Equations 33, 34
Shipment growth	20	% per year	Estimated from SAMA statistical data
Capital output ratio	3.5	dimensionless	Table 4.3
Growth rate of the output per man	1.2	% per year	Tables 2.2, 4.1
Salary growth rate	20	% per year	Previously explained
Price growth	0	% per year	Table 7.3
Propensity to consume	65	% per year	Table 7.3 note 1 and estimate below
GNP	120,000	million SR	Table 6.1

The behaviour of the system is obviously affected by the choice of the numerical values quantifying the parameters and the structural relationships of the model. This quantification procedure is inaccurate. A long-term model is mostly normative because it does not only deal with assumed changes in policy variables but with value as well as macro-structure changes which are quantified with a significant degree of uncertainty. However, the behaviour of a system dynamics model is much more dependent upon the existence and the sign of the feedback loops than upon the intensity of these loops, determined by the numerical values of both the parameters and the structural relationships of the model. Therefore, a high level of accuracy is not required except for the few key-parameters of the model. These parameters, which are determined through simulation experiments, are such that a small variation in their numerical value generates a very significant modification of the model behaviour. These parameters must consequently be estimated with precision.

Table 7.5: Exogenous Constants

Variable name	Symbol	Assumed value	Unit
Rate of exchange of the SR	ERSR	3.5	SR per US $
Maximum world oil demand to Saudi Arabia	MWD	5,454	m bbl/year
Decrease in world demand for oil per additional US $ in price	DWDA	181.8	m bbl/year
Number of man hours per year	NHW	1.76	thousand/year
Adjustment delay for desired import	AD	1	year
Adjustment delay for desired volume of non-oil production	ADD	2	year
Average duration of foreigners' labour contracts	ADFC	4	year
Capital depreciation rate	ROD	10	% per year
Adjustment delay for induced investment	ADE	4	year
Normal propensity to consume	MPCN	75	% per year
Normal exported proportion of expatriates' salaries	EPSN	60	% per year
Initial pilgrimage income	PILI	1,665	m SR/year
Computation time	DT	0.1	—

Table 7.6: Exogenous Tables

Exogenous variable	Table name	Assumed values (%)						
Rate of growth of import prices (Figure 5.2)	TRGIP	25	10	7.5	6	5	5	5
Rate of growth of pilgrimage income (Figure 6.10)	TRGPIL	10	6.6	4.2	2.7	1.5	0.7	0
Rate of return on financial assets (Figure 6.10)	RORTAB	6.5	6.5	6.5	6.5	6.5	6.5	6.5
	Time	1975	80	85	90	95	2000	05

The Structure of the Economic System

Table 7.7: Endogenous Tables

Involved variables	Table name	Assumed numerical values									
Discovery rate (% year)	DITAB	6	3.2	1.8	0.9	0.3	0				
Cumulative production (10^9 bbl)	(Figure 2.4)	25	50	75	100	125	150				
Energy output ratio (bbl/SR)	TEOR	.00167	.00167	.00167	.00167	.00167					
Capital per worker (10^3 SR)	(Figure 2.6)	50	75	100	125	150					
Growth rate of the world demand for oil (% year)	TRGWD	5.2	4.9	4.3	3.1	0					
Price of crude oil (US \$/bbl)	(Figure 2.7)	10	15	20	25	30					
Delay filling orders (consumers) (years)	TDFOC	5.5	3.2	2	1.25	1	0.8	0.6			
Inventory to consumer demand ratio (years)	(Figure 3.2)	0.5	0.75	1	1.25	1.5	1.75	2			
Delay filling orders (aut. inv) (years)	TDFOI	8	5.15	3.75	3	2.8	2.75	2.75			
Inventory to investor demand ratio (years)	(Figure 3.3)	0.5	0.75	1	1.25	1.5	1.75	2			
Delay filling orders (ind. inv.) (years)	TDFOI	8	5.15	3.75	3	2.8	2.75	2.75			
Inventory to investor demand ratio (years)	(Figure 3.3)	0.5	0.75	1	1.25	1.5	1.75	2			
Inventory multiplier (year)	TSTM	0.6	0.6	0.6	0.6	0.6	0.6	0.6	0.6	0.6	0.6
Shipment growth (% year)	(Figure 3.4)	0	2	4	6	8	10	12	14	16	18	20
Birth rate (% year)	BRTAB	4.8	4.4	4	3.75	3.5	3.4	3.2			
Real GNP per capita (1,000 SR)	(Figure 4.2)	20	25	30	35	40	45	50			
Death rate (% year)	DRTAB	2	1.48	1.2	1.04	1					
Wealth per capita (1,000 SR)	(Figure 4.3)	40	120	200	280	360					
Saudi labour output ratio (hours per SR of output)	SLORTAB	0.138	0.138	0.091	0.069	0.054	0.047	0.044	0.041		
Capital per capita (1,000 SR)	(Figure 4.5)	20	25	30	35	40	45	50	55		
Foreign labour output ratio (hours per SR of output)	TFLOR	0.05	0.05	0.045	0.042	0.04					
Capital per worker (1,000 SR)	(Figure 4.6)	50	75	100	125	150					
Capital output ratio	CORTAB	3.5	3.5	3.5	3.5	3.5	3.5	3.5			
Real GNP per capita (1,000 SR)	(Figure 4.8)	20	25	30	35	40	45	50			
Demand effect (%)	DEFTA	10	7	4.5	2.5	1.5	1	0.5	0		
Total supply to total demand ratio (%)	(Figure 5.3)	30	40	50	60	70	80	90	100		
Inflation multiplier	TINMUL	1	1	1	1	1	1	1	1		
Price growth (% year)	(Figure 6.2)	5	10	15	20	25	30	35	40	45	
Product availability multiplier	PATA	0.3	0.33	0.37	0.41	0.5	0.6	0.78	1		
Consumer supply to demand ratio	(Figure 6.3)	30	40	50	60	70	80	90	100		
Wealth multiplier	WMUTA	1	1	0.96	0.85	0.8					
Wealth per capita (1,000 SR)	(Figure 6.4)	40	120	200	280	360					
Product availability mult.	PAMUTA	1	1	0.99	0.98	0.96	0.92	0.87	0.8		
Consumer supply to demand ratio (%)	(Figure 6.7)	30	40	50	60	70	80	90	100		
Inflation multiplier	IMMUTA	1	1.01	1.02	1.04	1.05	1.08	1.09	1.1	1.1	
Price growth (% year)	(Figure 6.8)	5	10	15	20	25	30	35	40	45	
Proportion of foreign profits (% year)	PFPTAB	40	39	36	32	25	18	10	5	5	5
Saudi labour to total labour ratio (%)	(Figure 6.9)	10	20	30	40	50	60	70	80	90	100

Table 7.8: Constants of the Delays

Delayed variable	Delay type	Constant name	Assumed value (year)
Reserve production ratio	SMOOTH	DSR	3
Financial asset to GNP ratio	SMOOTH	DSRA	3
Productive capital per worker	SMOOTH	DSRR	5
Price of crude oil	SMOOTH	DSP	2
Imports	DELAY	IDEL	0.5
Shipment growth	SMOOTH	DSSG	2
Total shipments sent	SMOOTH	DSTS	2
Real GNP per capita	SMOOTH	DSGNP	5
Wealth per capita	SMOOTH	DSWPC	5
Productive capital per capita	SMOOTH	DSCPC	5
Net labour acquisition	DELAY	LCD	0.75
Autonomous capital acquisition	DELAY	ACAD	0.3
Induced capital acquisition	DELAY	ICAD	0.3
Price rate of growth	SMOOTH	DSPV	2
Total supply to total demand ratio	SMOOTH	DSRAT	2
Consumer demand	SMOOTH	DSCD	2
Consumer demand	DELAY	DIC	0.4
Consumer supply to demand ratio	SMOOTH	DSRT	2
Autonomous investment demand	SMOOTH	DSAID	2
Induced investment demand	SMOOTH	DSIID	2
Total demand	SMOOTH	DSDE	2
Growth of salaries and wages	SMOOTH	DSGSA	3
Investment income payments	DELAY	DEP	0.75
Return on financial assets	DELAY	RFAD	1

The behaviour of the model being highly dependent upon its feedback-loop structure, it is important not to omit any significant loop. Unfortunately, such an omission becomes more probable as the simulation period of the model is prolonged because a system's future does not only result from the dynamic evolution of its present structure but also from unforeseeable human factors such as social decisions or behavioural changes. Therefore, the model should not be regarded as a forecasting tool, that is, an action-orientated

The Structure of the Economic System

Table 7.9: Policies

Involved variables	Table name	Assumed numerical values						
Normal extraction rate (mbbl/year)	OILTAB	0	5	8	9	9	9	
Reserve production ratio (years)	(Figure 2.5)	0	10	20	30	40	50	
Absorption multiplier	TACMUL	1	1	1	1	1		
Financial asset to GNP ratio (years)	(Figure 2.5)	1	2	3	4	5		
Price multiplier	TOPMUL	1	1	1	1	1		
Price of crude oil (US $/bbl)	(Figure 2.5)	10	15	20	25	30		
Activity multiplier (% year)	TAM	26	26.5	27	28	30	32	35
Time	(Figure 4.4)	1975	1980	1985	1990	1995	2000	2005
Autonomous investment (billion SR/year)	TAINV	10	17.7	31.4	55.6	98.5	174.5	309.1
Time	(Figure 4.7)	1975	1980	1985	1990	1995	2000	2005
Government multiplier	GOTAB	1	1	1	1	1	1	1
Time	(Figure 6.5)	1985	1980	1985	1990	1995	2000	2005
Proportion of government help (% year)	PGHTAB	7	7	7	6.8	6.5	6.1	5.8
Time	(Figure 6.10)	1975	1980	1985	1990	1995	2000	2005

model, but as a planning tool, that is, a knowledge-oriented model. Given a scenario, i.e a sequence of possible events defined by the analyst and fed into the model, the model provides a clear and logical evaluation of the consequences of the simulated assumptions. This evaluation is general and not specific. The numerical value of a particular output at a particular date is less important than the overall trend of this variable, which is, itself, less important than the global behaviour of the model. Also, the evaluation of the results of the model is inseparable from the set of assumptions which has generated these results: the value of a model is wholly dependent upon the value of its assumptions.

PART II:
THE STRATEGIES OF ECONOMIC DEVELOPMENT

8 THE DEVELOPMENT PROCESS

What Type of Development?

Any global strategy of economic development is based upon political choices. Thus, Saudi Arabia is faced with two essential choices: the choice of the level of crude oil production and the choice of the type of economic development. These choices are essential because they determine the major future characteristics of the economy: achievements as well as constraints and problems. Although the first and especially the second Saudi Arabian Development Plans have explicitly opted for industrialization, the strategies of economic development analyzed in the second part of this book deal not only with this particular option but with important alternatives to industrial development. In addition, an important section is concerned with the policies regulating the oil sector: production policy as well as pricing policy. Also, the problems and constraints resulting from postulated strategies of development are thoroughly examined.

Table 8.1 presents the major strategies of development together with some of their positive and negative consequences. In order to define a reference for later analyses of the development strategies presented in Table 8.1, the initial simulation experiment, the numerical assumptions of which have been defined in Chapter 7, is based upon a postulated development programme that associates moderate industrialization and financial accumulation, and keeps the production of crude oil at its present level. The reference experiment can therefore be regarded as a rather pessimistic, conservative compromise which shows the major aspects and problems of several development options without explicitly privileging any of them. The major assumptions of the reference simulation can be summarized as follows:

In the Oil Sector:

production for export fixed at nine million barrels daily;
reasonable growth of the world demand for crude oil;
low substitution price (in a long-term perspective);
large potential reserves of crude oil;
no impact of the domestic development upon the production policy
   (ACMUL = OPMUL = 1).

Table 8.1: Problems and Advantages of the Major Development Strategies

Development Strategies	Problems	Positive Effects
Large production of crude oil	Surplus in financial resources Large investments abroad Economic dependence Effect of international and domestic inflation Rapid consumption of reserves	Large surplus in balance of payments Large financial resources for future domestic development No incentive to finding crude oil substitutes
Crude oil production based upon domestic needs	Possibility of oil shortages in the world International inflation	Moderate investments abroad Equilibrium between domestic development needs and financial resources Large oil reserves for future domestic usages Substantial increases in the price of crude oil and strong incentive to finding crude oil substitutes
Diversified industrialization	Large imports Effect of international inflation Large needs for expatriate labour Domestic inflation Balance of payment problem: high exported salaries and profits	Economic independence Strong economic development
Moderate industrialization International banking	Economic dependence. Possible insecurity International inflation	Large surplus in balance of payments Moderate needs for expatriate labour Moderate domestic inflation

In the Non-Oil Sector:

rapid growth of both the Saudi population and the Saudi labour force; substantial increase in the efficiency of the factors of production;

average yearly growth of 12 per cent in autonomous investment expenditures;
very significant long-term effect of inflation;
substantial return on financial assets;
large savings;
substantial payments abroad resulting from both the remittance of salaries and profits and a strong programme of international aid.

The Meaning of the Initial Simulation Experiment

It is important to correctly interpret the meaning of the reference simulation experiment. It must be clear to the reader that the purpose of this experiment is not to present an optimum programme of economic development, but to show clearly the way the economy works and how the problems are generated and interrelated. In other words, the fact that, in this simulation, several assumptions or results might be either underestimated or overestimated is not very important. What counts is the ability of the experiment to present the development problems in Saudi Arabia and to constitute a basis for further analyses and discussions (Chapter 9). One can easily understand after correctly identifying the source of a problem that the intensity of the problem as well as the probability to generate additional problems increases when the cause of this problem aggravates and smoothes when this cause gradually disappears, even if the intensity of the problem is not very precisely evaluated.

It is also important to underline the fact that this model is a long-term model which is not concerned with short-term policies or regulation programmes. The analysis of the long-term behaviours generated by the model may suggest the implementation of short-term regulation policies in order to correct or modify the long-range trend of given variables, but in its present state the model cannot include such policies. The purpose is, in fact, to identify long-term economic behaviours as a function of long-term policy decisions. For example, a usual long-term behaviour is a cyclical growth of the output. The exponential or linear trend of the output is superimposed with a cycle that results from the fact that the gap between the desired and the actual state of the economic system alternatively widens and narrows. It is economically desirable to iron this cycle out through monetary or fiscal policies. These policies, however, cannot be anticipated in a long-term perspective but are implemented as soon as the recession phase of the short-term cycle is identified. As a result, the simulation experiments conducted with the model sometimes lead

108   *The Strategies of Economic Development*

to sub-optimum performances in the short term. It is important to understand that these sub-optimum performances, which result from long-term phenomena, can usually be corrected in the short term. However, these corrections cannot be introduced in the model because the simulation experiments cannot be interrupted. A solution to this problem, which is dependent upon the flexibility of the simulation language, is presented in the conclusion of the book.

Production and Pricing of Crude Oil

The changes in the major variables of the oil sector are shown in Figures 8.1 and 8.2. As previously mentioned, the combination of the

Figure 8.1: Results of Reference Simulation: Oil Sector

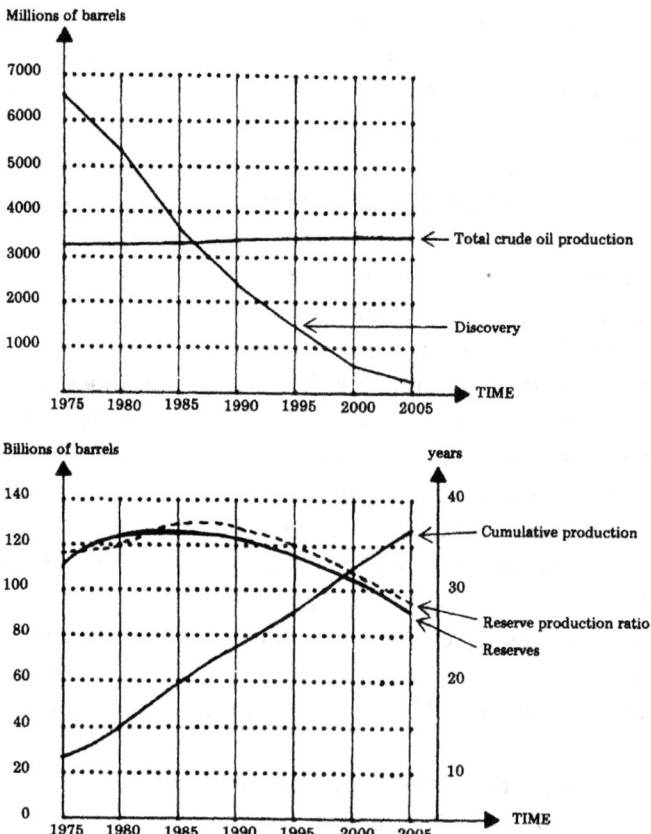

The Development Process

Figure 8.2: Results of Reference Simulation: Oil Sector

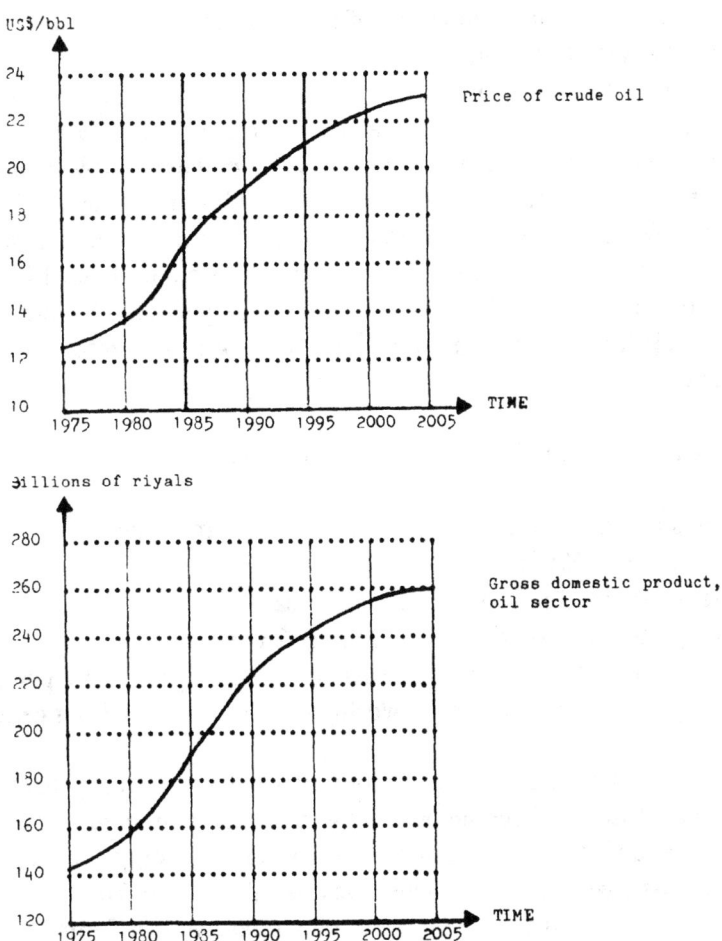

assumptions regarding the normal rate of crude oil production and the rate of discovery results in a constant production for export of nine million barrels daily. Until 1986, crude oil discoveries are greater than production. Therefore, both the level of oil reserves and the reserve production ratio grow. At the end of the simulation period, in 2005, the reserve production ratio is twenty-eight years which corresponds to ninety billion barrels of remaining crude oil reserves. Cumulative production grows from twenty-six billion barrels in 1976 to one hundred and twenty-six in 2005. As a result, from 1976 to 2005, one hundred billion barrels have been produced and seventy-nine have been discovered. A similar result would have been obtained with the same production rate and no discovery if the initial level of petroleum reserves had been set at 190 billion barrels in 1975. This result is quite consistent with recent estimations of both probable and possible present reserves in the kingdom.

The combined effect of a constant production for export and an assumed growth of the world demand for crude oil at an average annual rate of about four per cent results in a moderate growth in the price of crude oil which increases from 12.4 US $ a barrel in 1975 to 23.2 in 2005. This corresponds to an average growth of two per cent per year. The increase in the gross domestic oil product, from 143 billion riyals in 1975 to 260 in 2005, is entirely generated by the growth in price. The average annual rate of growth is therefore two per cent.

The above results can be summarized as follows:

constant production for export: 9 million barrels daily;
reserves in 2005: 90 billion barrels;
reserve production ratio in 2005: 28 years;
average annual growth of the oil price: 2 per cent;
average annual growth of the gross domestic oil product: 2 per cent;
average annual growth of the world demand for oil: 4.3 per cent.

These results are, of course, quite conservative. It is assumed that crude oil substitutes become progressively available in increasing quantity and that the transition to new sources of energy occurs in an inflationless environment. It is also assumed that Saudi Arabia is willing and able to maintain large petroleum reserves for future domestic usage. The major interest of this scenario (which is significantly modified later in this book) is to evaluate Saudi Arabia's domestic development possibilities when it is supposed that the long-term contribution of crude oil to the domestic development is limited.

The Non-Oil Production

The behaviour of the non-oil sector is shown in Figures 8.3, 8.4, 8.5 and 8.6. Figure 8.3 deals with the human resources of the kingdom. The Saudi population, assumed to be five million in 1975, reaches eleven million in 2005, which corresponds to an average annual rate of growth of 2.6 per cent. The Saudi labour force, from 1.3 million in 1975, grows to 3.7 million in 2005 at an average rate of 3.4 per cent per year. The substantial progress in the efficiency of the Saudi labour

The Development Process

Figure 8.3: Results of Reference Simulation: Population and Labour Force

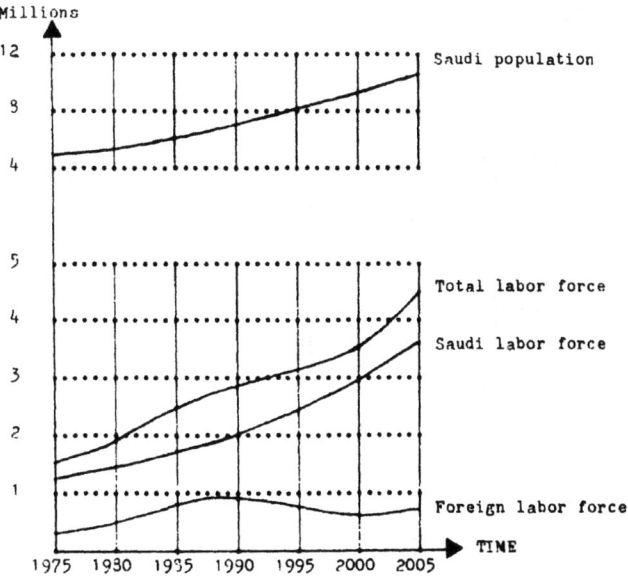

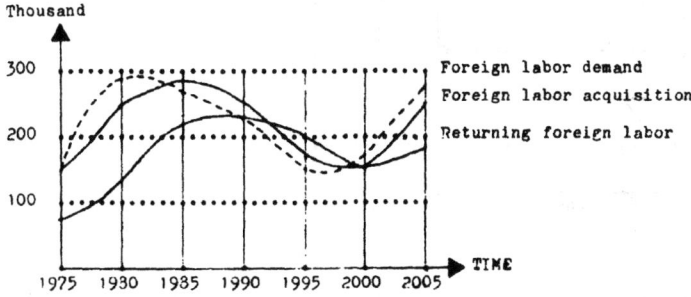

force, assumed to triple in less than fifteen years, results in a moderate demand for foreign labour. The level of foreign labour force rises from 314,000 in 1975 to 945,000 in 1991, decreases to 650,000 in 2000 and rises again to 783,000 in 2005. In 1991, the year when the level of foreign labour force reaches a maximum, Saudi labour constitutes 69 per cent of the total labour force. This proportion increases to 83 per cent in 2005. Labour acquisition reaches a maximum in 1985 with 284,000 imported labourers which corresponds to an average monthly acquisition of 23,700.

From 1975 to 2005, the volume of productive capital accumulates

112 The Strategies of Economic Development

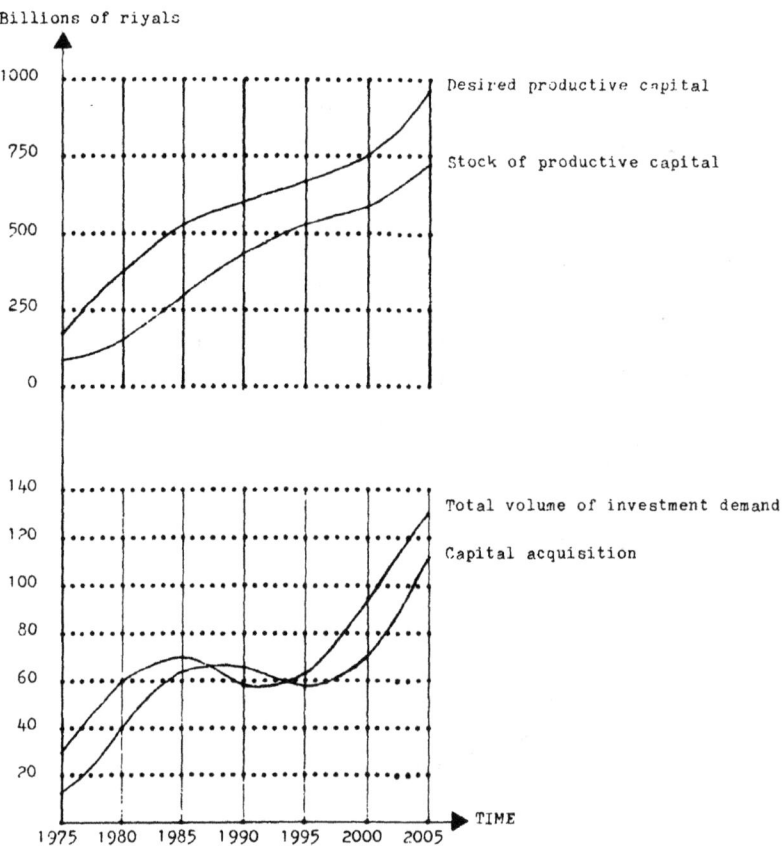

Figure 8.4: Results of Reference Simulation: Productive Capital Accumulation

at an average annual rate of 6.1 per cent (Figure 8.4) from 115 billion riyals in 1975 to 726 in 2005. There are, however, as shown in Figure 8.4, several phases of growth. Although the autonomous investment demand is steadily growing at an average annual rate of twelve per cent, the difference between desired and actual capital, which is constantly growing from 1975 to 1985, decreases from 1985 to 1993, which results in an induced decrease in the induced investment demand. The seven-year recession that the economy is then experiencing results from a stabilization taking place after a phase of overgrowth. This stabilization period, which can be avoided through short-term policy decisions aimed at stimulating total demand (for example a larger increase in the volume of autonomous investment or governmental consumption expenditures), ends in 1993 when sharper

Figure 8.5: Results of Reference Simulation: Non-Oil Production

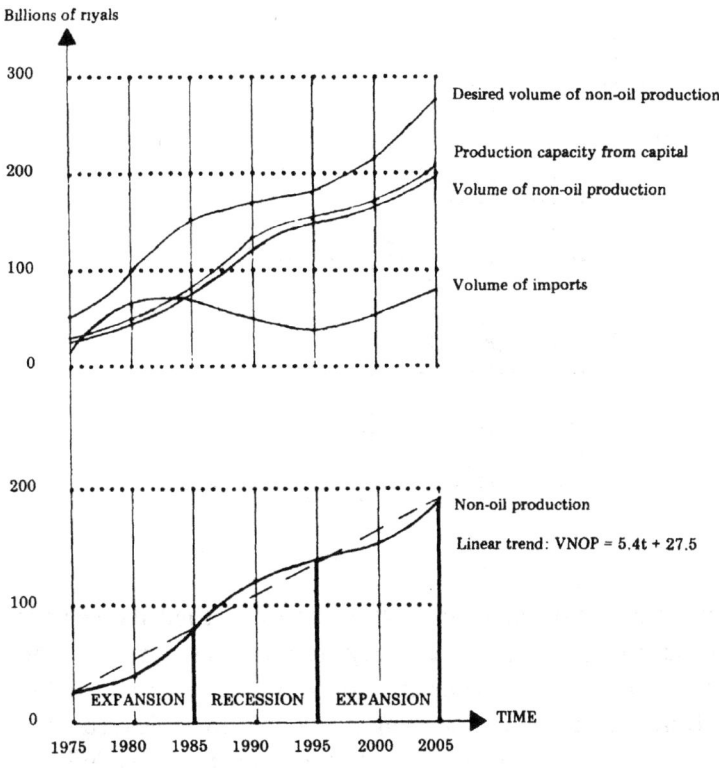

growth resumes (Figure 8.4). The diagrams of Figure 8.4 also show the effect of the various delays affecting the process of capital accumulation. There is a four-year delay between desired and actual capital and an additional three-year delay between demand and capital acquisition.

Figures 8.5 and 8.6 illustrate the process of non-oil production. This process is controlled by the labour force: there exists a continuous surplus of productive capital which varies from twenty per cent in 1975 to six per cent in 2005. This capital surplus makes productive capital the most abundant factor so that the actual volume of non-oil production is determined by the production capacity from the labour force. Non-oil production grows from twenty-eight billion riyals in 1975 to 195 in 2005 at an average annual rate of 6.5 per cent. As was indicated previously, the cyclical fluctuations of non-oil production that are superimposed on a long-range linear trend (Figure 8.5) result from a continuous adaptation of

114   *The Strategies of Economic Development*

Figure 8.6: Results of Reference Simulation: Inventory

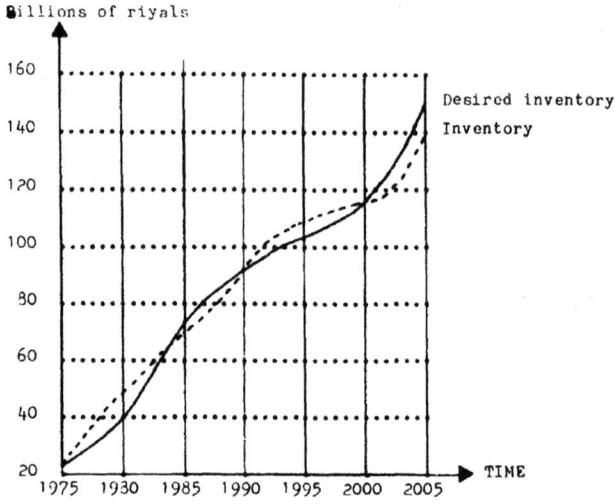

the actual state of the economic system to the desired state and can be avoided through short-range anticyclical policies. Similarly, the gap between desired non-oil production and actual non-oil production results from various delays adapting the system to its desired state.

The volume of imports oscillates between twenty-three billion riyals in 1976 and eighty-three in 2005. Imports decrease during the

Figure 8.7: Results of Reference Simulation: Supply Demand Ratios

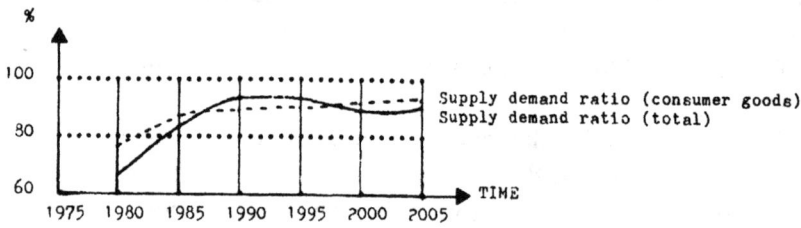

1985–1994 period which corresponds to the phase of recession of the economic system. Imports grow again from 1995 onwards. From 1977 to 1984, imports are greater than non-oil production. Imports constitute fifty-nine per cent of total supply in 1976, fifty per cent in 1985, twenty-three per cent in 1995, and thirty-one per cent in 2005.

Figure 8.8: Results of Reference Simulation: Supply and Demand

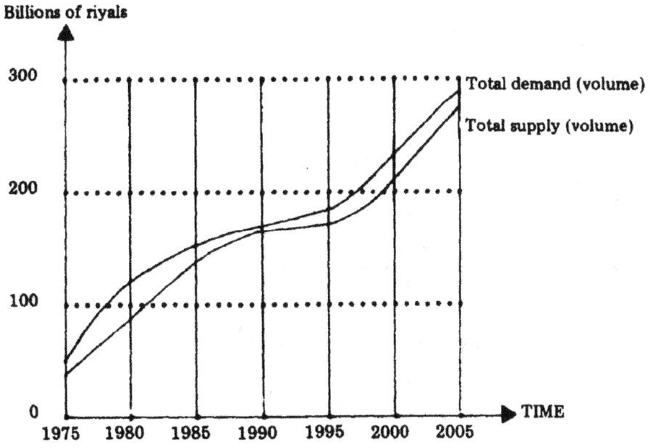

Figures 8.7 and 8.8 show that the delays supplying the economic system with goods and services are progressively reduced as the economy develops. The global supply demand ratio varies from sixty-one per cent in 1978 to ninety-six per cent in 1991 and ninety-one per cent in 2005. The volume of both supply and demand follows the general trend of the economy. Total demand reaches 293 billion riyals in 2005, that is, 150 per cent of the volume of non-oil production, and total supply 271 billion riyals. From 1975 to 2005, total demand grows at an average annual rate of six per cent and total supply at an average rate of 6.5 per cent.

The Accumulation of Financial Assets

It has been previously indicated that the results of the reference simulation concerning the oil sector were conservative. It is also the case of the non-oil sector. The diagram of Figure 8.9 shows that from 1975 to 2003 the economy does not utilize the totality of its financial capacity for productive investment purposes which results in a positive surplus and a continual accumulation of financial assets. The oscillations of both the net surplus and the stock of financial assets follow the general trend of the economy: the recession phase of the economic system corresponds to a period of relative saturation in domestic absorption and gives rise to an increase in the net surplus. From 2003 onwards, a period of time which is situated in the second phase of sharp economic growth, the economy experiences a growing deficit in current financial resources (negative surplus) which is

116 *The Strategies of Economic Development*

Figure 8.9: Results of Reference Simulation: Surplus and Financial Assets

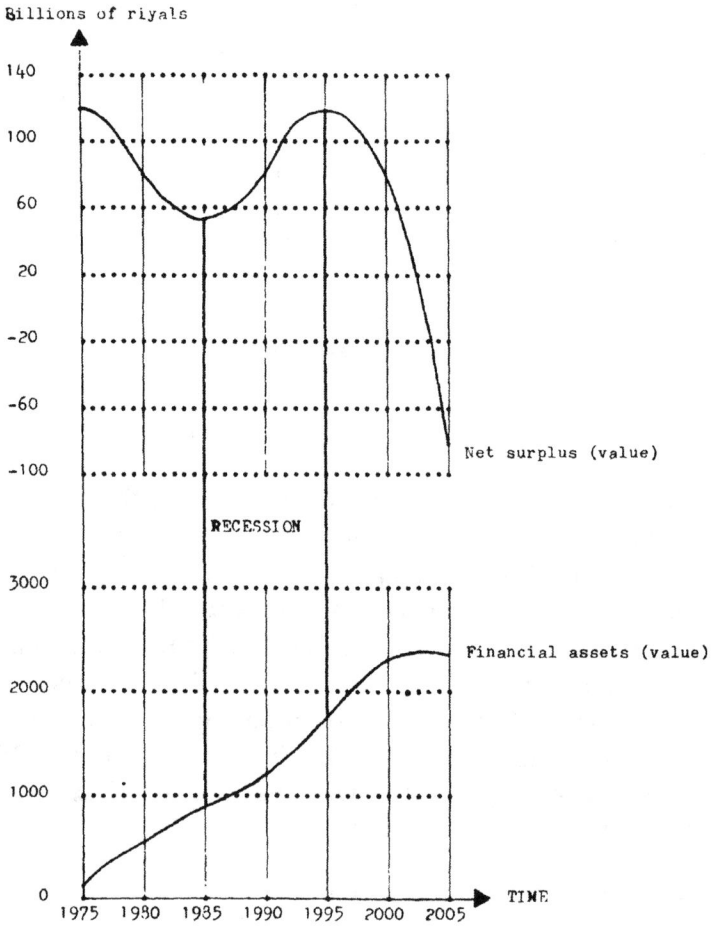

Figure 8.10: Results of Reference Simulation: Ratio of Financial Assets to GNP

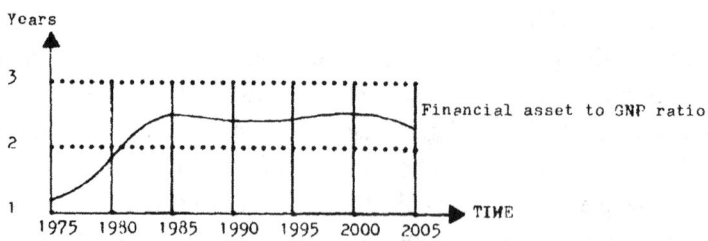

The Development Process

compensated through a rapidly growing repatriation of the Saudi funds invested abroad. The combined effects of inflation and a growing demand for investment funds deplete the financial assets in twelve years: if the simulation experiment is continued after 2005, the value of the stock of financial assets becomes nil in 2015. From 1975 to 2003, however, the value of the stock of financial assets grows from 139 billion riyals to 2442, at an average annual rate of 10.4 per cent. Furthermore, from 1981 to 2005, the financial assets are constantly greater than twice the gross national product of the corresponding years (Figure 8.10).

The Impact of Inflation

The impact of inflation can be clearly seen comparing Figure 8.9 to Figure 8.11. The diagram of Figure 8.11 shows the changes in the volume of total capital (productive and financial) which increases from 254 billion riyals in 1975 to 1,242 in 2005 at an average annual rate of 5.3 per cent. As the average annual rates of growth of the volume of productive capital and the value of the financial assets are respectively 6.1 per cent and 9.6 per cent, there exists a significant annual rate of inflation. This rate is plotted in Figure 8.12. Figure 8.13 shows the changes in the price index which reaches 4.6 in 2005. The average annual rate of inflation is consequently five per cent.

Figure 8.11: Results of Reference Simulation: Volume of Produtive and Financial Capital

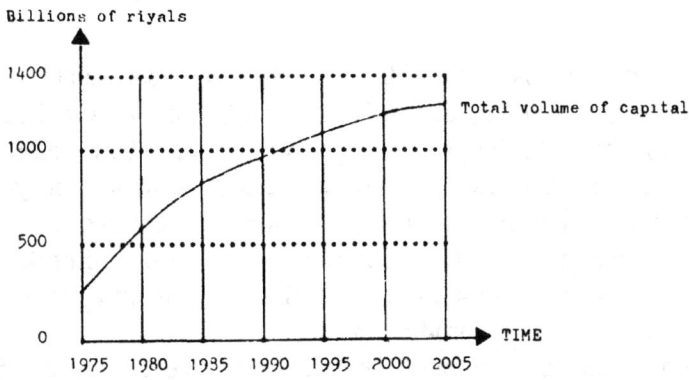

Although the assumptions of the model regarding inflation are very conservative compared to the present situation, it is clear that inflation is one of the major constraints to the Saudi Arabian economic

Figure 8.12: Results of Reference Simulation: Price Rate of Growth

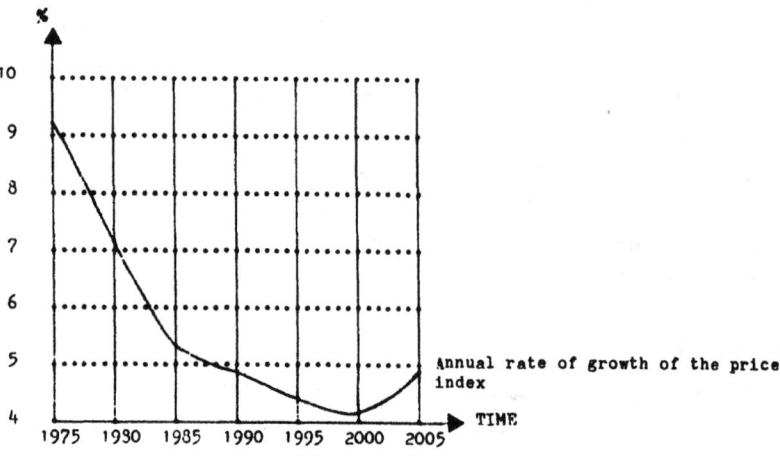

Figure 8.13: Results of Reference Simulation: Price Index

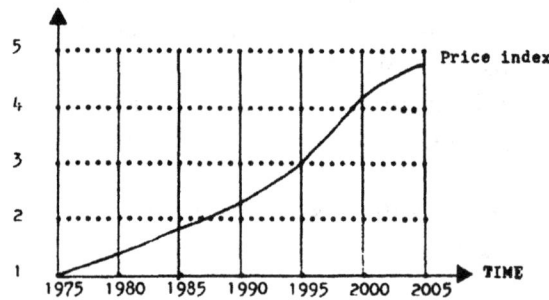

development. The real value of the financial assets accumulated abroad is particularly affected by domestic inflation (Figure 8.9 and 8.11) which, together with the problem of economic dependence, insecurity and international inflation, constitutes a strong incentive to recycle as much financial resource as possible within the economic system. There is, however, a limit to domestic absorption which, if broken through, increases the inflation rate. In this case, the ultimate solution is a decrease in crude oil production.

The dynamic equilibrium of the Saudi Arabian economy is in fact dependent upon the relative values of the domestic absorption rate and the rate of generation of oil revenues. The complexity in the management of the economy results from the fact that the second rate does not only depend upon domestic factors but involves the market for

The Development Process

crude oil at a world level. As a result, it exists now and it might exist in the future a substantial discrepancy between these rates that might lead, if both domestic and international inflation are not significantly reduced, to a substantial decrease in Saudi Arabian crude oil production and subsequently to a new energy crisis.

The Gross Domestic Product

Figure 8.14: Results of Reference Simulation: Gross Domestic Product

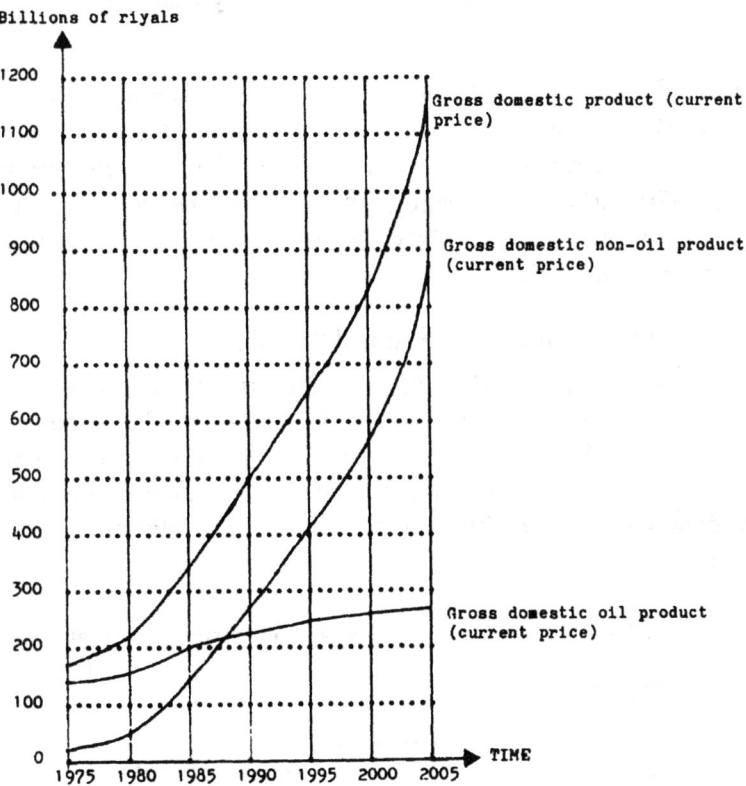

The changes in the gross domestic product are analyzed in Figure 8.14 and in the table on page 120 which also gives the average annual rates of growth of the components of the gross domestic product.

The low rate of growth of the gross domestic product in volume partly results from the assumption that the production of crude oil is constant. The growth of the output is also significantly affected by the inflation rate which multiplies the cost of economic development by an increasing factor. It is obvious that the rate of growth of domestic production can be much higher (Chapter 9), but, as was previously explained, the purpose of this experiment is not to define the maximum value of the rate of growth of the Saudi Arabian domestic production.

	Value	Volume
GDP	6.3 per cent	1.3 per cent
Oil sector	2 per cent	0
Non-oil sector	11.8 per cent	6.5 per cent

Figure 8.14 shows that from 1987 to 2005 the non-oil sector contributes more than the oil sector to domestic production. This contribution grows from sixteen per cent in 1975 to twenty-four per cent in 1980, forty-two per cent in 1985, fifty-six per cent in 1990, sixty-three per cent in 1995, sixty-nine per cent in 2000 and seventy-seven per cent in 2005.

The Distribution of the Gross National Product

As shown in Figure 8.15, the value of the gross national product increases from 161 billion riyals in 1975 to 1,148 in 2005 at an average annual rate of 6.5 per cent. The long-range trend of the gross national product is consequently almost identical to the long-range trend of the gross domestic product which implies a dynamic equilibrium in the balance of payments.

Figure 8.15: Results of Reference Simulation: Gross National Product

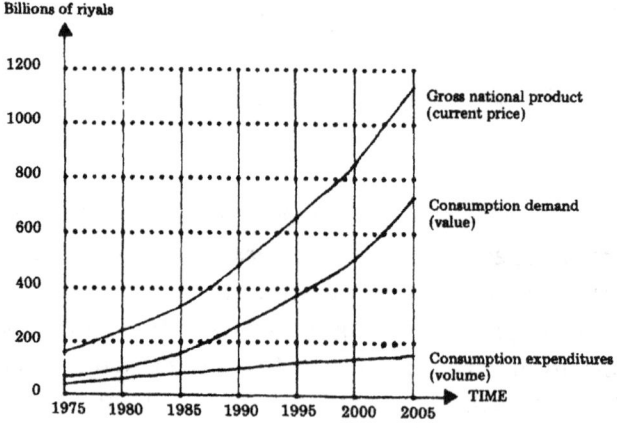

The Development Process

In this experiment, the economy is characterized by a substantial rate of saving (the propensity to consume only reaches sixty-seven per cent in 2005) which contributes to generate the positive surplus and the large accumulation of financial assets shown in Figure 8.9.
A higher level of consumption expenditures would accelerate domestic absorption and productive capital accumulation, but also would stimulate domestic inflation.

The distribution of the gross national product is shown in Figure 8.16. Salaries and wages, including exported salaries, increase from twenty-eight billion riyals in 1975 to 803 in 2005 at an average annual rate of 11.4 per cent. Such a high rate of growth results from the assumption that salaries and wages are totally indexed on inflation, an assumption that can be modified through policy decisions. In 2005, salaries and wages after payments abroad constitute sixty-four per cent of the gross national product, a proportion that is comparable to the present situation in developed countries.

Figure 8.16: Results of Reference Simulation: Salaries and Profits

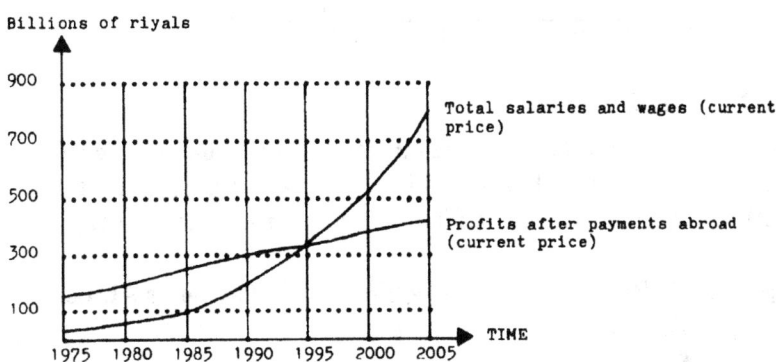

As shown in Figure 8.17, the average annual salary grows from 17,180 riyals in 1975 to 177,420 in 2005 at an average annual rate of about eight per cent which results from both the inflation rate (five per cent) and the average annual rate of growth in productivity (three per cent). The rate of growth of total salaries and wages is consequently the result of the following changes:

inflation:	5 per cent
productivity:	3 per cent
average annual salary:	8 per cent
total labour force:	3.4 per cent
salaries and wages:	11.4 per cent

122   *The Strategies of Economic Development*

Figure 8.17: Results of Reference Simulation: Average Salary and Output per Man

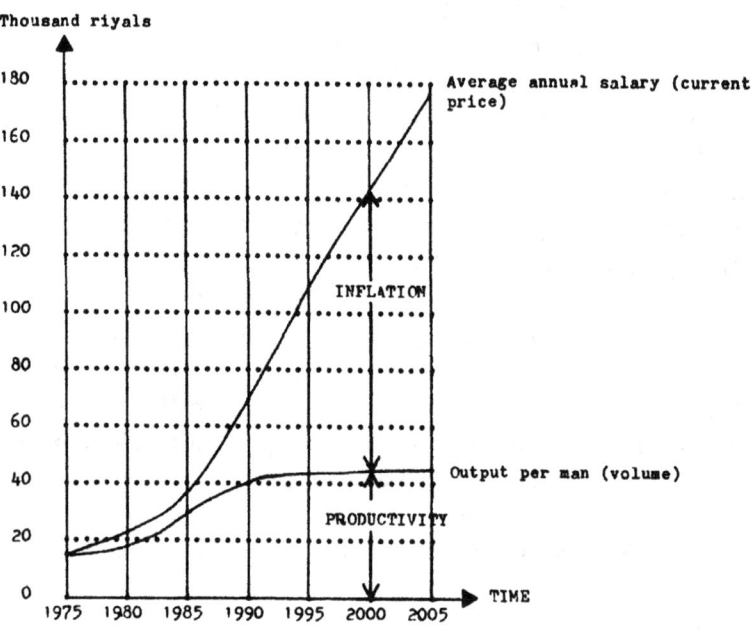

The Balance of Payments

As shown in Figure 8.18, net payments abroad oscillate between a maximum value of 29 billion riyals in 1991 and a minimum of − 30 billion in 2001. The Saudi Arabian balance of payments is

Figure 8.18: Results of Reference Simulation: Payments Abroad

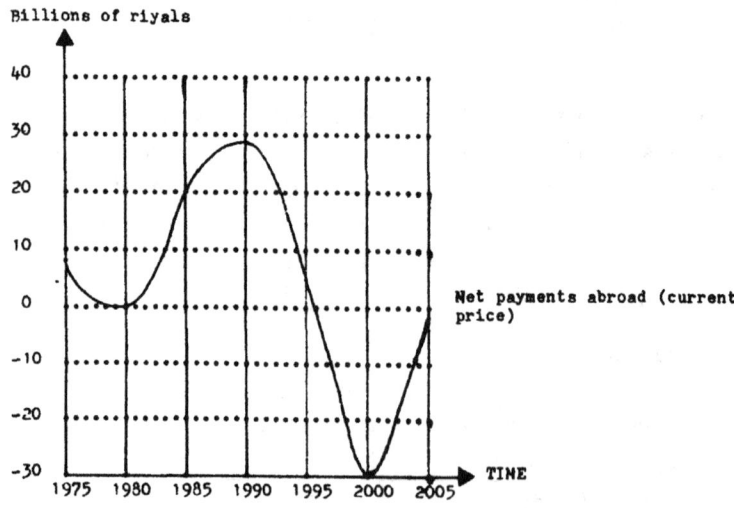

The Development Process

Figure 8.19: Results of Reference Simulation: Balance of Payments

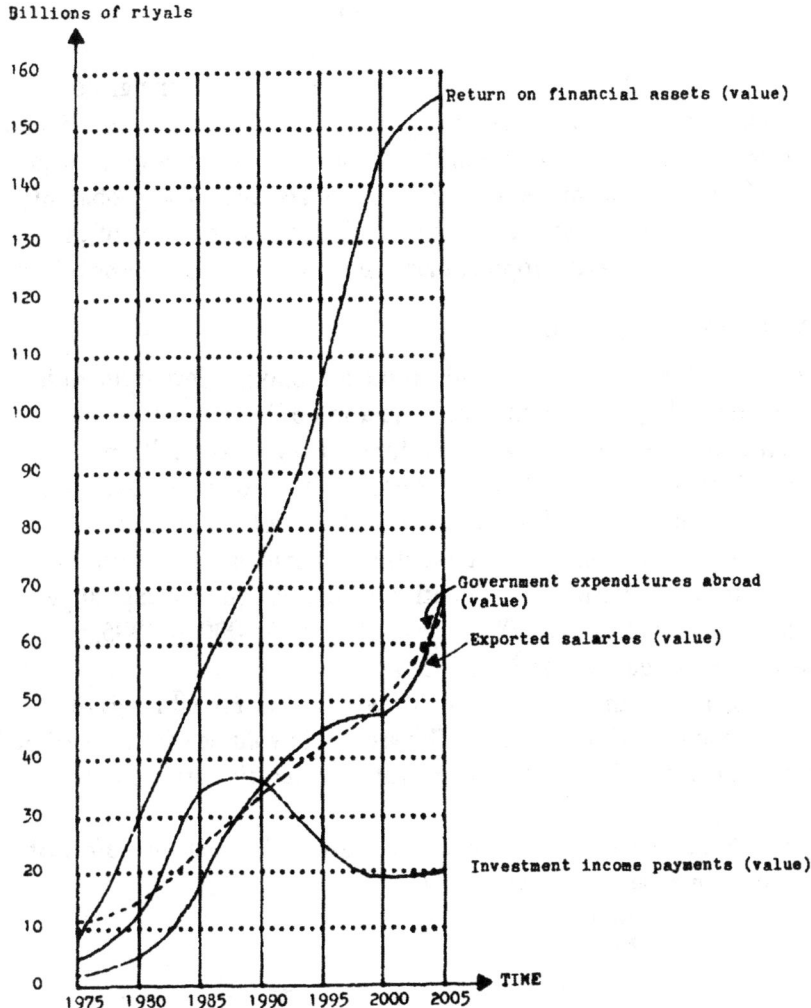

therefore roughly in equilibrium from 1975 to 2005. The economy is able to compensate for the high cost of both the foreign labour force and its substantial international aid through large returns on financial assets (Figure 8.19). In 2005, the situation is as follows:

return on financial assets	:	156 billion riyals (13.6 per cent of GNP)
exported salaries	:	69 billion riyals (6 per cent of GNP)
exported profits	:	21 billion riyals (1.8 per cent of GNP)

expenditures abroad : 67 billion riyals (5.8 per cent of GNP)
total expenditures : 157 billion riyals (13.6 per cent of GNP)

Payments abroad constitute a significant proportion of the gross national product. This situation might lead Saudi Arabia to implement policies aimed at restricting remittances as well as decreasing foreign aid in order to limit monetary and financial leakages. The probability of this option grows with the rate of domestic development of the economy since this development also generates increasing expenditures.

The Per Capita Indicators

Figure 8.20 shows that the Saudi Arabian economic development is characterized by a substantial accumulation of both financial and productive assets per capita. The volume of the total wealth per capita increases from 51,000 riyals in 1975 to 126,000 in 2005 at an average annual rate of three per cent. Total wealth per capita primarily results from the accumulation of financial assets and also from the accumulation of productive capital. Productive capital per capita increases from 23,000 riyals in 1975 to 63,000 in 2005 at an average annual rate of 3.3 per cent.

Compared to the accumulation of wealth, the annual flows of production per head is modest. The growth in volume of gross national product is just sufficient to compensate the negative effects of

Figure 8.20: Results of Reference Simulation: General Indicators of Economic Development

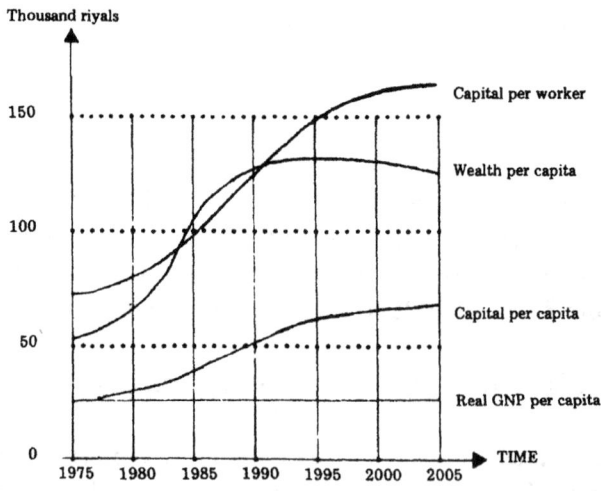

The Development Process

inflation and the impact of population growth. As a result, real gross national product per capita stays constant from 1975 to 2005. This result emphasizes again the very significant negative effect of inflation on the long-term economic development: inflation distorts the entire economic structure and permanent efforts to control it are of utmost importance (see Chapter 9).

The 2005 Balance Sheet of the Economy

The major performances of the economic system during the analyzed thirty-year period are grouped in Table 8.2, which shows the average annual rate of growth, first in volume and then in value, of selected variables of the model.

Table 8.2: Results of Reference Simulation: Summary

	%	%
Crude oil production	—	—
Price of crude oil	—	2
Gross domestic product	—	2
World demand for oil	4.3	—
Saudi population	2.6	—
Saudi labour force	3.4	—
Total labour force	3.4	—
Inflation	—	5
Productive capital	6.1	11.1
Autonomous investment	7	12
Non-oil production	6.5	11.5
Inventory	6.2	11.2
Total demand	6	11
Total supply	6.5	11.5
Financial assets	4.6	9.6
Total capital	5.3	10.3
Gross domestic non-oil product	6.5	11.8
GDP	1.3	6.3
GNP	1.5	6.5
Consumption	3.2	8.2
Productivity	3	8
Average annual salary	3	8
Total salaries and wages	5.4	11.4
Total profits	—	4
Productive capital per capita	3.3	8.5
Wealth per capita	3	8
GNP per capita	0	5

These performances lead to the following balance sheet, established for the year 2005 in billion riyals. The results of this experiment, which omit all human and social development as well as significant aspects of national wealth such as residential land, other consumer durables and other natural resources (particularly natural gas) are not satisfactory. Their major justification is to prove that the solution to the development problem in Saudi Arabia is not obvious although the kingdom is financially rich and owns massive amounts of valuable natural resources. The next chapter demonstrates that the development process analyzed in this experiment is indeed sub-optimum and can be largely improved.

	Value	Volume
Reserves of crude oil	7,280	7,280
Productive capital	3,318	726
Financial assets	2,359	516
Inventory	640	140
2005 GNP	1,148	251
TOTAL	14,745	8,913
Population (millions)	10.7	10.7
Wealth per capita (riyals)	1,378,037	832,991

9 THE MANAGEMENT OF THE ECONOMIC DEVELOPMENT

The previous chapter was purposely based upon a rather pessimistic view of the development process in order to identify clearly both the problems of this development and their origins. This chapter is aimed at analyzing the major development problems and evaluating the economic consequences of positive solutions to these problems. To simplify the analysis, the method primarily consists of comparing the balance sheets of the final year of the simulation experiments as well as the assumptions that have generated these results. In addition, the major economic trends are commented upon.

Structural Improvement of the Model

There are two assumptions of the model that have to be modified. The first involves the substitution price for crude oil and the second deals with the analysis of consumption.

It is unrealistic to consider a constant substitution price for crude oil in a long-term approach. As indicated previously, the substitution price is affected by the net rate of inflation which is assumed to be totally exogenous to the model. In order to take this new assumption into consideration, the initial formulation:

$$SP.K = SMOOTH\left(\frac{MWD}{DWDA} - \frac{COPEX.K}{(DWDA)(1 + RGWD.K)}t\right)$$

is replaced by the following system of equations:

$$SP.K = SMOOTH(PRICE.K)$$

$$PRICE.K = SUP.K - \frac{COPEX.K}{(DWDA.K)(1 + RGWD.K)}t$$

$$SUP.K = (SUPI)(1 + RGSUP)^t$$

$$DWDA.K = \frac{3{,}200}{SUP.K - 12.4}$$

with SP = smoothed price of crude oil; PRICE = price of crude oil; SUP = substitution price; SUPI = initial substitution price; and RGSUP = exogenous annual rate of growth of the substitution price.

The equation which defines DWDA is estimated from the initial Saudi Arabian crude oil production and the initial price of crude oil according to the analysis presented in Chapter 2. The numerical value of the constants SUPI and RGSUP is defined later in this chapter.

The second modification is concerned with the treatment of consumption expenditures. In order to improve the accuracy of the balance sheet of the economy, the initial assumption that all consumption goods are immediately destroyed by the consumption process is replaced by a more disaggregated analysis: there are two categories of consumption goods, consumer durables and non-durable goods. Consumer durables accumulate into a stock that contributes to the total wealth of the economy. The corresponding equations are as follows:

$$CCAP.K = CCAP.J + (DT)(CDAC.JK - CDDEP.JK)$$
$$CDAC.KL = (PCD)(SSC.JK)$$
$$CDDEP.KL = CCAP.K/ADCD$$

with CCAP = stock of consumer durables; CDAC = acquisition of consumer durables; PCD = proportion of consumer durables in total consumption expenditures; CDDEP = depreciation of consumer durables; and ADCD = average duration of consumer durables.

In addition, the equation for total capital (TCAP) is written:

$$TCAP.K = CAP.K + CCAP.K + (FINAS.K/PRIND.K)$$

and it is assumed that the numerical value of the constants is defined as follows:

CCAP initial	:	25 billion riyals
PCD	:	30 per cent
ADCD	:	15 years.

Development Costs: Inflation

Inflation was identified in Chapter 8 as one of the major costs, or even the major cost, of the economic development. As shown in Figure 5.1, there are two main causes which generate inflation: the exogenous growth of import prices; and the discrepancy between supply and demand which results from the rigidity of the economic system. In addition, there exists an induced cause, the salary effect, which depends upon the above factors.

The Management of the Economic Development

In order to evaluate the cost of inflation, the assumptions controlling the above variables are modified as follows: the exogenous growth of import prices is reduced as indicated in Figure 9.1. Also, the various delays adapting supply to demand are corrected (Table 9.1 and Figure 9.2) and the intensity of the demand effect is attenuated (Figure 9.3).

Table 9.1: Modification of the Delays Adapting Supply to Demand

Constants	Reference Value	Present Value
Import delay	0.5 (6 months)	0.25 (3 months)
Labour acquisition delay	0.75 (9 months)	0.5 (6 months)
Capital depreciation	10 per cent	5 per cent

Figure 9.1: Annual Rate of Growth of Import Prices: Modified Assumption

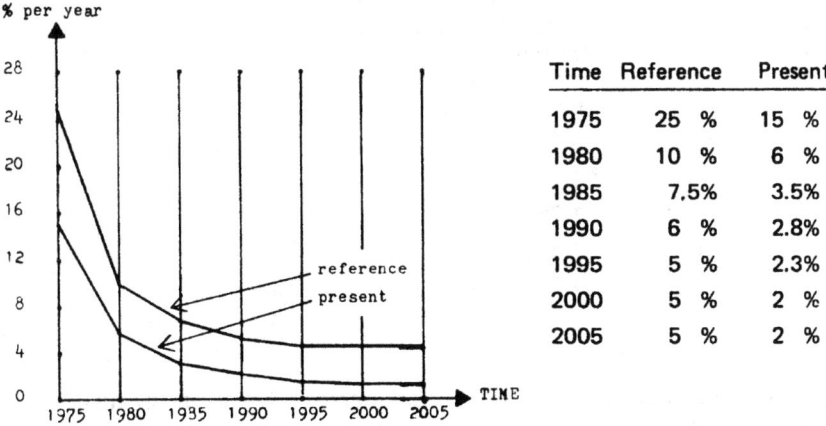

Time	Reference	Present
1975	25 %	15 %
1980	10 %	6 %
1985	7.5%	3.5%
1990	6 %	2.8%
1995	5 %	2.3%
2000	5 %	2 %
2005	5 %	2 %

With this modified set of assumptions, two simulations were conducted. The first experiment (Experiment A) includes the above and below modifications except the change in the delay filling orders from consumers which keeps its reference value (Figure 9.2). The second experiment (Experiment B) includes all changes shown in Table 9.1, Figures 9.1, 9.2 and 9.3. The reason for this two-fold experiment is that a shorter delay filling orders from consumers generates two contradictory effects: it attenuates inflation through a

Figure 9.2: Delay in Filling Orders from Consumers: Modified Assumption

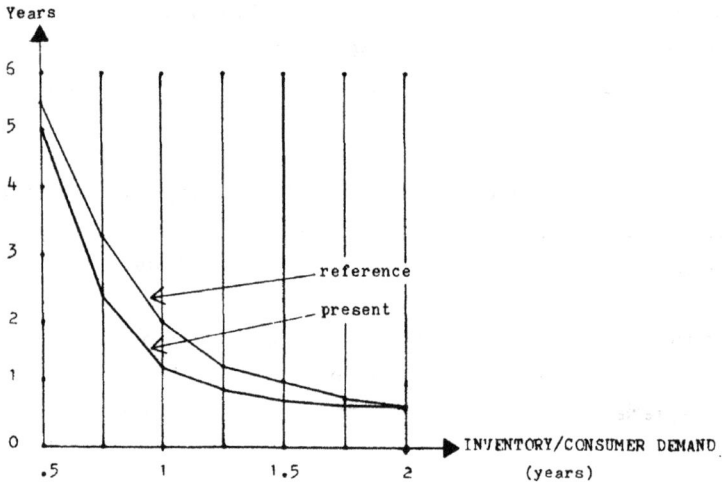

Inventory/ consumer demand	Delay Reference	Present
0.5	5.5	5
0.75	3.2	2.4
1	2	1.25
1.25	1.25	0.9
1.5	1	0.7
1.75	0.8	0.6
2	0.6	0.6

better supply/demand ratio but it also increases inflation through the stimulation of consumer demand, the availability of goods and services being improved.

As shown in Figure 9.4, the rate of inflation is, in both experiments, sensibly reduced. The average annual value of this rate is 3.2 per cent in Experiment A, 3.5 per cent in Experiment B compared to an average annual rate of five per cent in the reference experiment. This long-term decrease in the inflation rate significantly improves the general behaviour of the economy as illustrated in Figure 9.5. The average annual rate of growth in volume of the various indicators are modified as shown in the table on page 132.

The Management of the Economic Development   131

Figure 9.3: Demand Effect on Inflation: Modified Assumption

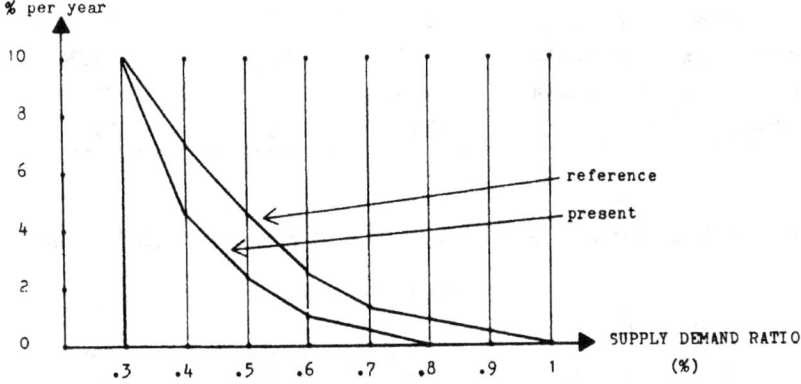

Supply/ demand ratio	Reference	Present
0.3	10%	10%
0.4	7%	4.5%
0.5	4.5%	2.5%
0.6	2.5%	1.2%
0.7	1.5%	0.7%
0.8	1%	0
0.9	0.5%	0
1	0	0

Figure 9.4: Changes in Price Index with Modified Assumptions

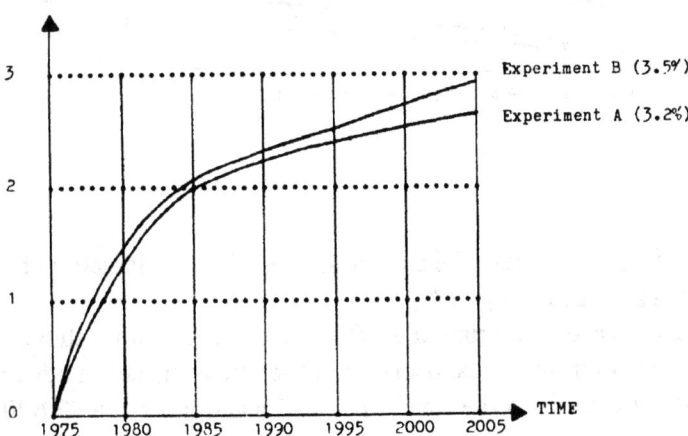

Indicators	Reference	Experiment A	Experiment B
Real GNP per capita	0	1.3%	1%
Productive capital per worker	2.6%	2.7%	2.75%
Productive capital per capita	3.3%	4%	4%
Wealth per capita	3%	5.6%	5.2%

Figure 9.5: Changes in Per Capita Indicators with Modified Assumptions

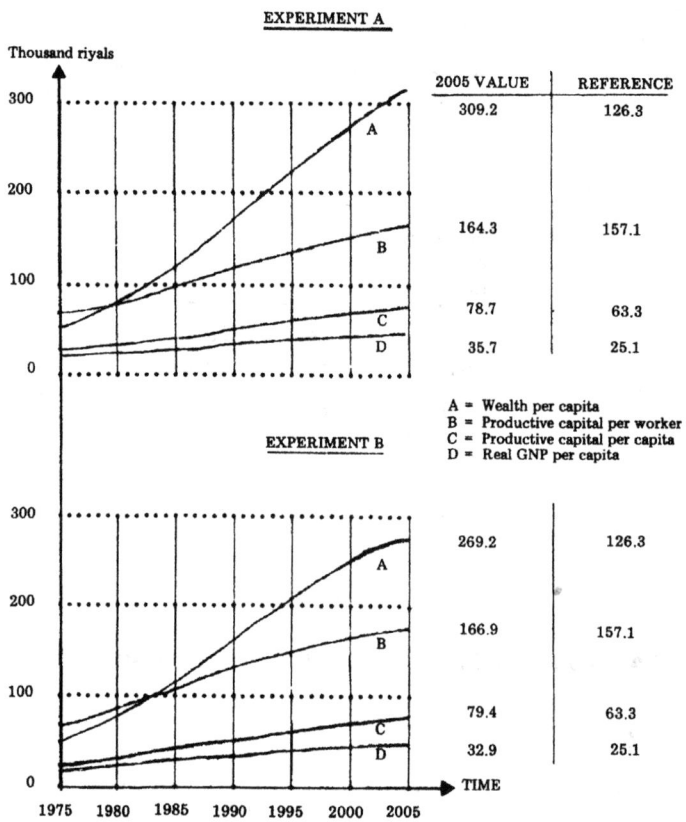

The 2005 balance sheet of the economy in volume is largely bettered (see table at head of page 133).

On the basis of Experiment A, the balance sheet shows that a 1.8 per cent average annual decrease in the rate of inflation adds more than 200,000 riyals to the wealth per capita and more than 2,600

	Reference (million riyals)	Experiment A (million riyals)	Experiment B (million riyals)
Reserves of crude oil	7,280	7,290	7,040
Productive capital	726	1,079	1,080
Consumer durables	n.a.	458	496
Financial assets	516	2,231	1,626
Inventory	140	170	165
2005 GNP	251	402	366
TOTAL	8,913	11,630	10,773
Population (millions)	10.7	10.9	10.9
Wealth per capita (riyals)	832,991	1,066,972	988,349

billion riyals to the volume of national wealth. In other words, one can roughly say that each one per cent increase in the average annual rate of inflation generates for the total economy a total cost of 1,500 billion riyals, i.e. 19 billion barrels of crude oil at the 2005 price. This long-term, cumulative cost is variable because the relationship inflation:cost is not linear. Thus, the optimum performance of the economic system, which is obtained when both the import effect and the demand effect are supposed to be inactive, is an average annual rate of inflation of half a per cent which leads to the following 2005 balance sheet in volume:

Reserves of crude oil :	7,055 billion riyals
Productive capital :	1,700 billion riyals
Consumer durables :	662 billion riyals
Financial assets :	4,005 billion riyals
Inventory :	259 billion riyals
2005 GNP :	598 billion riyals
Total	14,279 billion riyals
Population (millions) :	9.6
Wealth per capita :	1,487,396 riyals

Compared to the reference run, the economic return is then more than 5,300 billion riyals and the cumulative cost of each one per cent increase in the rate of inflation is 1,200 billion riyals.

These impressive results should, of course, be interpreted in relation with the assumptions that have generated them and should not be considered accurate estimates. These numbers, however, provide a basis to assess the very high inflation costs and entirely justify the previous remarks about the utmost importance of an inflationless economic development. This analysis also permits the reader to evaluate the economic consequences of greater inflation rates. As the cost of each additional per cent in the inflation rate increases when this rate rises, a higher rate of inflation would generate a cumulative cost greater than estimated in the above analysis. For example, a ten per cent average annual rate of inflation during the analyzed thirty-year period would probably cost Saudi Arabia between 15,000 and 20,000 billion riyals or even more. The conclusion is clear: the economy simply cannot afford high, long-term inflation rates.

Development Costs: Payments Abroad

Another significant source of domestic expenditure is the debit side of the balance of payments. There are three major categories of expenditure: salary remittances, investment income payments and government expenditure abroad. Except the last category, it is unlikely that this expenditure can be significantly reduced through either changes in economic behaviour or policy decisions leading to a larger domestic utilization of these funds. Such policy decisons would, on the contrary, discourage both foreign labour and foreign capital that the kingdom needs and welcomes in order to achieve both the domestic growth and the technology transfers that its development requires. The solution to the problem is therefore at least to compensate for these payments by the returns on financial assets. The equilibrium of the balance of payments, which depends upon domestic inflation, the ability of the kingdom to manage its financial reserves and the global rate of domestic development, is achieved in the reference simulation experiment. The cumulative deficit in the balance of payments is about 250 billion riyals only in 2005 (Figure 8.18). The reduction of the inflation rate (Experiment A) substantially improves the international financial situation of the kingdom and generates a large cumulative surplus (Figure 9.6). This surplus results from the fact that the returns on financial assets are large enough to more than cover the expenditures which are, however, much larger than in the reference experiment since a reduction in the inflation rate significantly stimulates the economic development and, subsequently, the demand for factors of production, particularly foreign

The Management of the Economic Development 135

labour.

It is interesting to remark that a further decrease in the rate of inflation deteriorates the situation illustrated in Figure 9.6. Figure 9.7, obtained with the assumption that both the import effect and the demand effect are nil, illustrates this case. The reason is that, as the rate of inflation decreases, the domestic development as well as the induced demand for factors of production, which determine most of the payments abroad, grow faster than the returns on financial assets, which, themselves, decrease when more financial resources are recycled within the national economy. Table 9.2 illustrates this process. This point is important. It demonstrates that the solution to a problem calls for changes in behaviours and/or policies which, themselves, generate other problems. This phenomenon results from

Figure 9.6: Payments Abroad: Experiment A

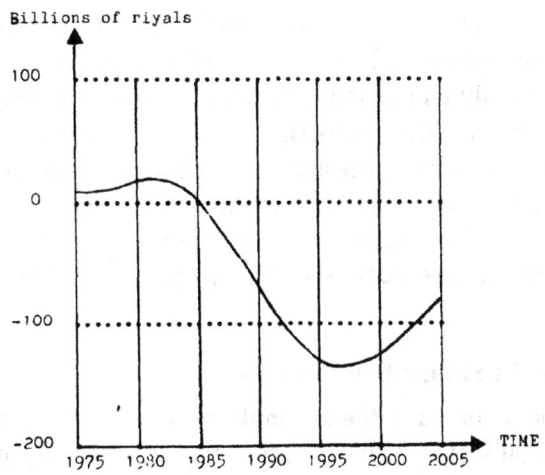

Figure 9.7: Payments Abroad: Inflationless Environment

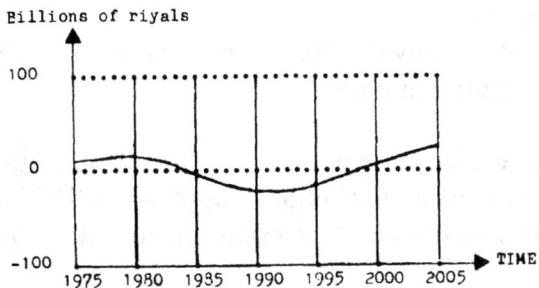

Table 9.2: Effect of Inflation on Labour Demand (thousand) and Payments Abroad (billion riyals)

Time	Foreign labour force			Return on financial assets		
	Reference	Experiment A	Inflation-less environment	Reference	Experiment A	Inflation-less environment
1975	314	314	314	9	9	9
1980	524	723	738	30	28	27
1985	948	743	838	54	65	55
1990	944	442	564	74	132	111
1995	799	548	572	104	216	186
2000	650	1,200	1,185	144	295	253
2005	783	2,428	2,413	156	368	296

the fact that the economy is a system and not a juxtaposition of independent mechanisms. The fundamental concept of this research is the concept of dynamic, non-linear interrelations between economic and social variables which, in social sciences, must substitute for static, linear analyses based upon the assumed independence of phenomena. In terms of system dynamics, the modification in net payments abroad shown in Figure 9.7 is explained by the fact that a positive loop, which involves the total economy, is progressively getting an opposite polarity.

Crude Oil and Economic Development

It is now time to abandon the assumptions of the reference experiment regarding the oil sector. The simulation experiment analyzed in this paragraph, which is based upon a quite different view of the policy decisions regulating the oil sector, includes the following modified assumptions:

> initial reserves: 300 billion barrels
> no discovery
> annual rate of growth of the substitution price of 2.5 per cent
> initial substitution price: 25 US $/bbl

These assumptions imply an initial reserve production ratio of ninety-four years and a substitution price of 54 US $/bbl in 2005. In addition, it is assumed that the maximum normal extraction rate is twenty million barrels daily and varies as shown in Figure 9.8. This rate, which defines the postulated maximum Saudi Arabian production capacity for export, is corrected by the price multiplier based upon an initial level of production of 3,200 million barrels per year. Thus, the initial price multiplier is:

$$\frac{3,200}{(20)(365)} = 0.44$$

and is assumed to vary as shown in Figure 9.9.

Figure 9.8: Normal Extraction Rate: Modified Assumption

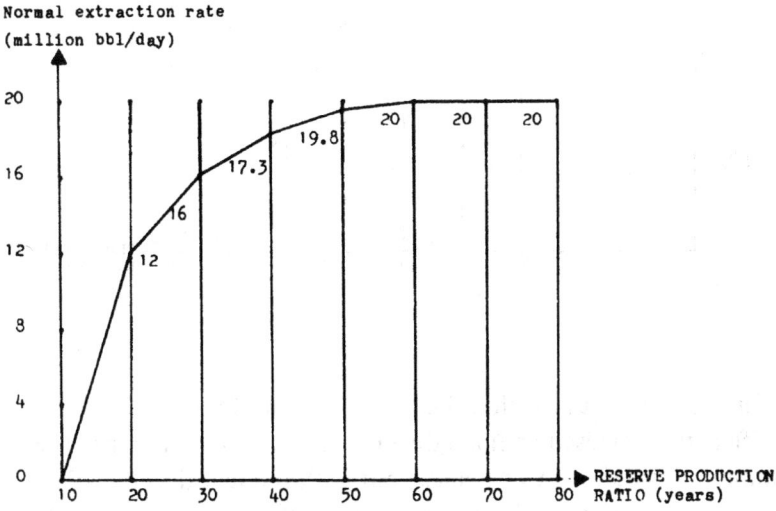

Figure 9.9: Price Multiplier: Modified Assumption

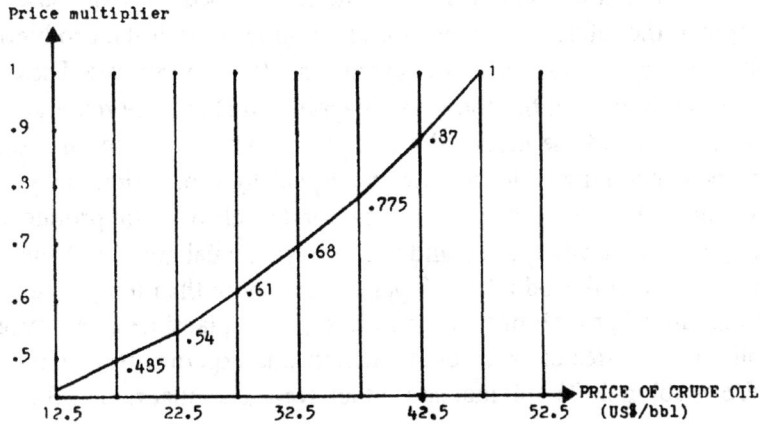

138 *The Strategies of Economic Development*

Figure 9.10: Growth of World Demand: Modified Assumption

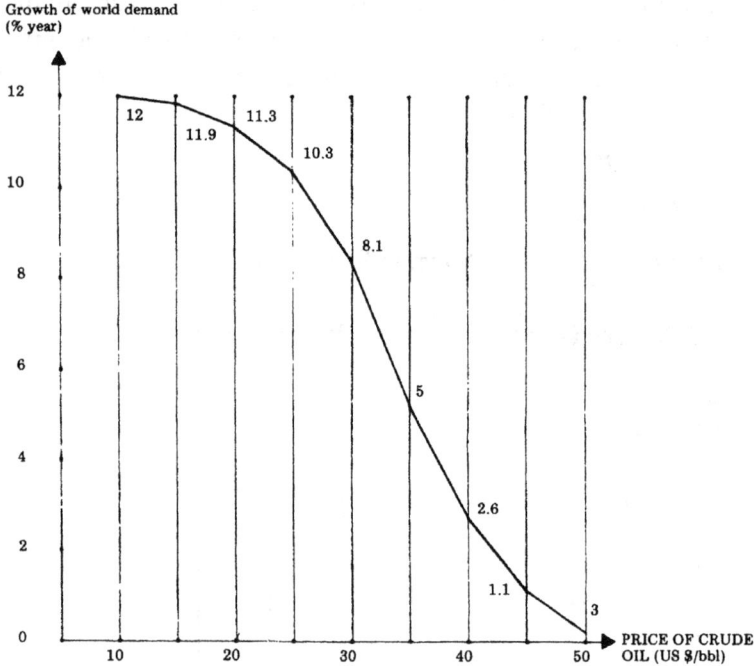

Finally, it is assumed that the world demand for crude oil is significantly increased compared to the reference experiment. The assumption is defined to be consistent with the fact that the 1976 OPEC production was 11.7 per cent up on 1975 (see Figure 9.10).

The simulation experiment analyzed below combines the above modified assumptions in the oil sector and the assumptions of Experiment A in the non-oil sector. The first consequence of these changes in the reference assumptions is to modify both the production and the price of crude oil as well as the final level of reserves. These changes are shown in the following diagrams. It should be remarked that the results of the modified assumptions in the oil sector are still conservative as far as both pricing and especially production are concerned. One hundred and thirty billion barrels only are produced during the thirty-year period and the average annual growth of the gross domestic oil product is 4.7 per cent. A more than ten per cent average annual growth of this product is a quite plausible assumption. Similarly, the price of crude oil, which, in this experiment, reaches 36 US $/bbl in 2005 and increases at an average annual rate of 3.5

per cent, could grow at a faster rate (five to eight per cent annually) especially as the world demand progressively substitutes Saudi Arabian crude oil for other sources of supply as a result of the gradual consumption of their reserves. Furthermore, even at 36 US $ a barrel, crude oil is still inexpensive compared to the downstream products manufactured from it which are currently sold well above US $ 100 a barrel.

Figure 9.11: Production of Crude Oil

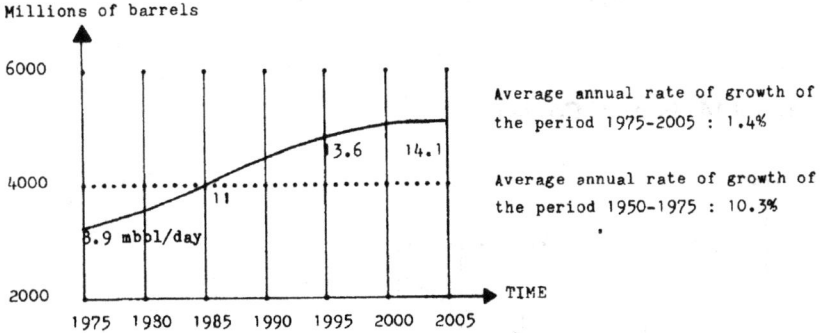

Figure 9.12: Reserves of Crude Oil and Cumulative Production

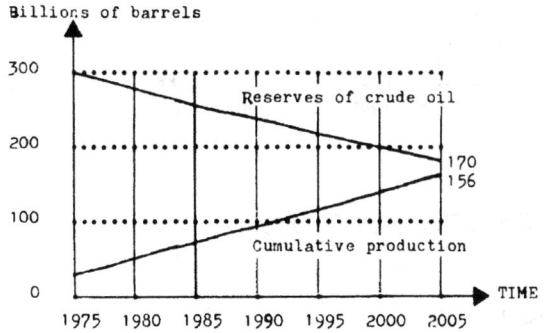

The second consequence of the modified assumptions is to stimulate domestic development of the economy through successive increases in income flows. The volume of non-oil production reaches 324 billion riyals in 2005, which corresponds to an average annual rate of growth of 8.3 per cent (this rate was 7.9 per cent with the assumptions of Experiment A). The average annual rate of inflation is a moderate 3.1 per cent. As the assumption regarding the autonomous

140   *The Strategies of Economic Development*

Figure 9.13: Reserve Production Ratio

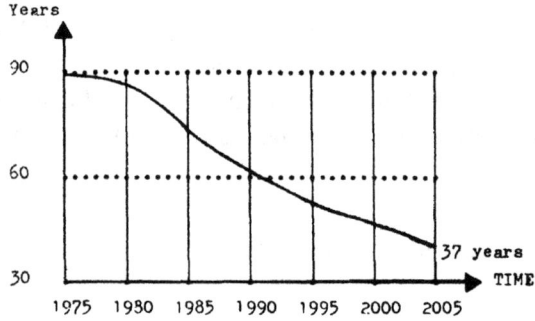

Figure 9.14: Price of Crude Oil

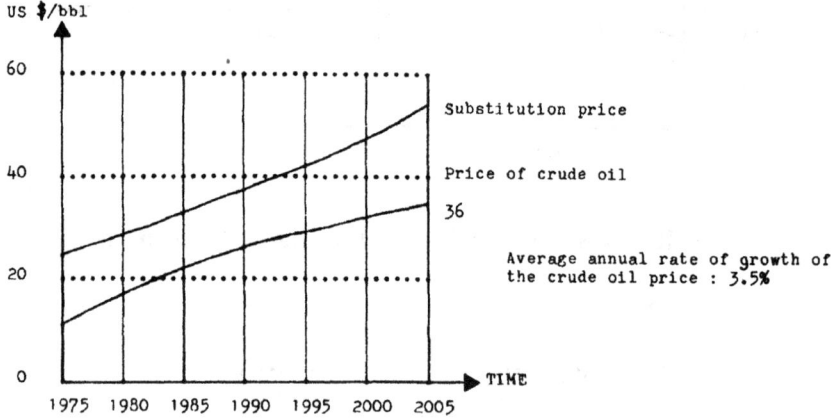

Figure 9.15: Gross Domestic Oil Product

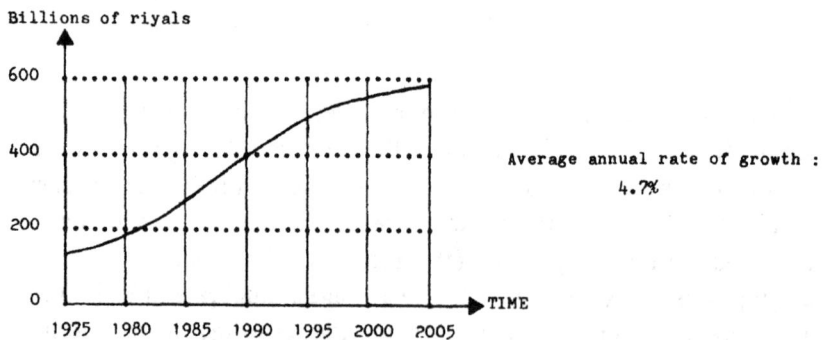

investment policy is not modified, the growth in the volume of non-oil production only results from increases in both consumption demand and induced investment which only absorb a small amount of the additional revenues. As a result, the net surplus largely rises (Figure 9.16) and generates a massive 9,800 billion riyal level of financial assets in 2005 (current price), i.e. a sixty per cent increase on Experiment A. This level, together with productive capital and the gross national product, largely raises the wealth per capita as shown in Figure 9.17.

Figure 9.16: Net Surplus

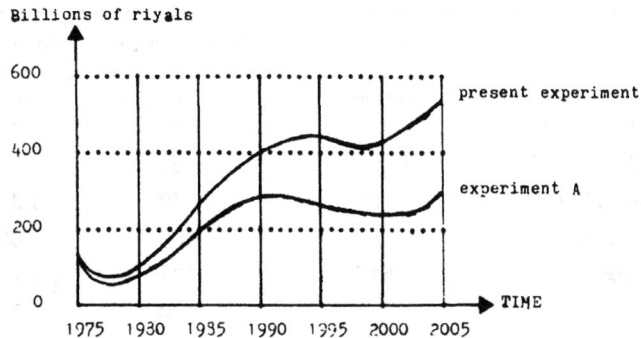

Figure 9.17: Indicators of Economic Development

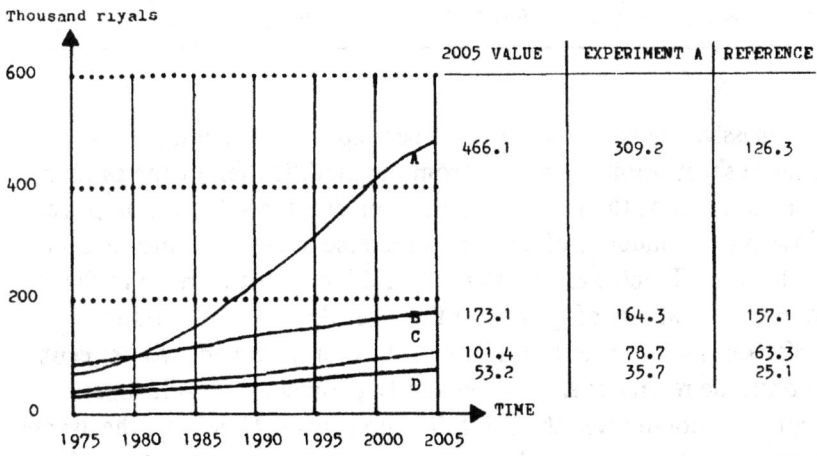

A = wealth per capita
B = capital per worker
C = capital per capita
D = real GNP per capita

Indicators	Reference	Experiment A	Present Experiment
Real GNP per capita	0	1.3%	2.6%
Productive capital per worker	2.6%	2.7%	2.9%
Productive capital per capita	3.3%	4 %	5 %
Wealth per capita	3 %	5.6%	7.2%

2005 Balance Sheet of the Economy (Volume): Compared Experiments

	Reference (billion riyals)	Experiment A (billion riyals)	Present Experiment (billion riyals)
Reserves of crude oil	7,280	7,290	21,375
Productive capital	726	1,079	1,316
Consumer durables	n.a.	458	605
Financial assets	516	2,231	3,793
Inventory	140	170	216
2005 GNP	251	402	579
TOTAL	8,913	11,630	27,884
Population (millions)	10.7	10.9	10.2
Wealth per capita (riyals)	832,991	1,066,972	2,736,459

The massive increase in the wealth per capita shown in the above balance sheet primarily results from the modification of the assumptions concerning the reserves of crude oil and the substitution price. However, the induced effects of an increase in crude oil production in the non-oil sector are substantial. A 2.7 per cent increase in the average annual rate of growth of the gross domestic oil product (this rate is 4.7 per cent in the present experiment and two per cent in both the reference simulation and Experiment A) results in an additional non-oil wealth of 2,200 billion riyals. Moreover, the average economic return per barrel of crude oil, in terms of generation of non-oil wealth, rises. In the reference simulation, a cumulative production of 100 billion barrels of crude oil was associated with a non-oil wealth in volume of 1,633 billion riyals, that is, an average wealth of 16.3

riyals per barrel produced. The decrease in the inflation rate (Experiment A) resulted in a 4,340 billion riyal non-oil wealth for the same cumulative production of crude oil, that is, an average wealth of 43.4 riyals per barrel produced. In the present experiment, the cumulative production of crude oil is 130 billion barrels and the non-oil wealth is 6,510 billion riyals. The average wealth per barrel produced is consequently 50.1 riyals. It is interesting to note that the present experiment with no inflation would lead to the following non-oil wealth:

productive capital	:	2,280 billion riyals
consumer durables	:	917 billion riyals
financial assets	:	7,145 billion riyals
inventory	:	359 billion riyals
2005 GNP	:	987 billion riyals
Total	:	11,688 billion riyals

that is, 89 riyals per barrel produced. As, for a given production capacity, the economic cost of inflation obviously increases when the level of activity rises, the above result shows that it is much more preferable to raise the level of crude oil production when the general economic conditions of the non-oil sector are favourable.

Government Expenditures and Economic Development

The previous experiments have emphasized the first major problem of the Saudi Arabian economic development which is inflation. Both the cost and the negative effects of inflation have been analyzed in detail and the economic returns of inflationless development processes have been evaluated. This paragraph is based upon the assumption that the inflation problem is solved. Our present purpose is to analyze the positive and negative effects of a faster, inflationless rate of domestic development. This analysis modifies the assumptions of the previous experiments as follows: first, the price multiplier in the oil sector is supposed to grow faster as the price of crude oil approaches the substitution price (Figure 9.18). Second, the autonomous government expenditure in investment goods (AINV) are increased. Five experiments with an average annual rate of growth in autonomous investment demand respectively equal to twelve per cent, fourteen per cent, sixteen per cent, eighteen per cent and twenty per cent, have been conducted. All other assumptions are not modified. Consequently, this experiment combines the above modified assumptions with the assumptions of the simulation experiment analyzed in the fourth paragraph of this chapter.

Figure 9.18: Price Multiplier: Modified Assumption

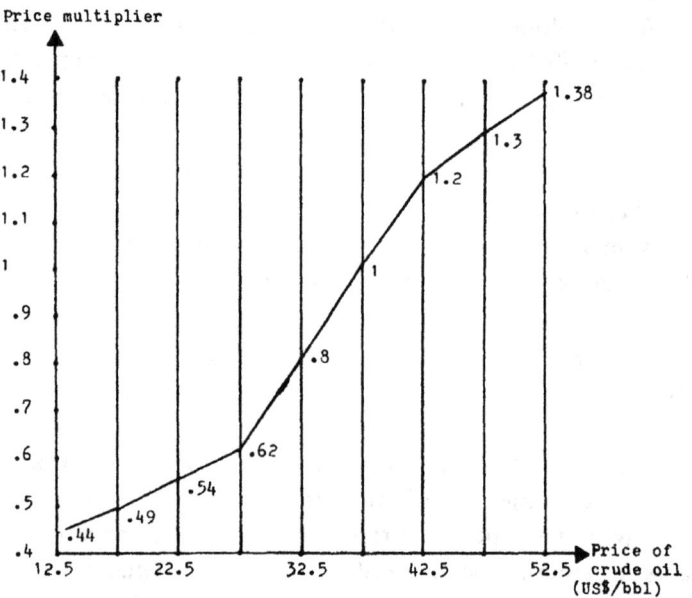

The present simulation experiments clearly illustrate the second major problem of the Saudi Arabian economic development which is the supply of labour force. As soon as the domestic conditions of the non-oil sector allow the economy to increase its rate of development, a moderate increase in this rate generates a large demand for foreign labour and, subsequently, very substantial payments abroad. For example, with a sixteen per cent average annual rate of growth in autonomous investment, the average growth of the kingdom's output is:

	Value	Volume
Gross domestic non-oil product	12.8%	9.3%
Gross domestic oil product	5.2%	2 %
Gross domestic product	8 %	4.7%
Gross national product	7.7%	4.5%

and the average annual growth rate of the foreign labour force is 10.2 per cent. These growth rates mean that, in order to increase the volume of non-oil production from 27.5 billion riyals in 1975 to 433 in 2005, the economy must accumulate a stock of 6,300,000 foreign labourers. The 2005 labour situation of the kingdom is as follows:

Saudi population	:	10,171,000
Saudi labour force	:	3,637,800
Foreign labour force	:	6,289,000
Total labour force	:	9,926,800

The changes in the population and labour sector are shown in Figure 9.19. The immediate consequence of these massive requirements in foreign labourers is a very substantial increase in the payments abroad (Figure 9.20) which reaches 234 billion riyals in 2005, and the fact that the gross domestic product grows faster than the gross

Figure 9.19: Population and Labour

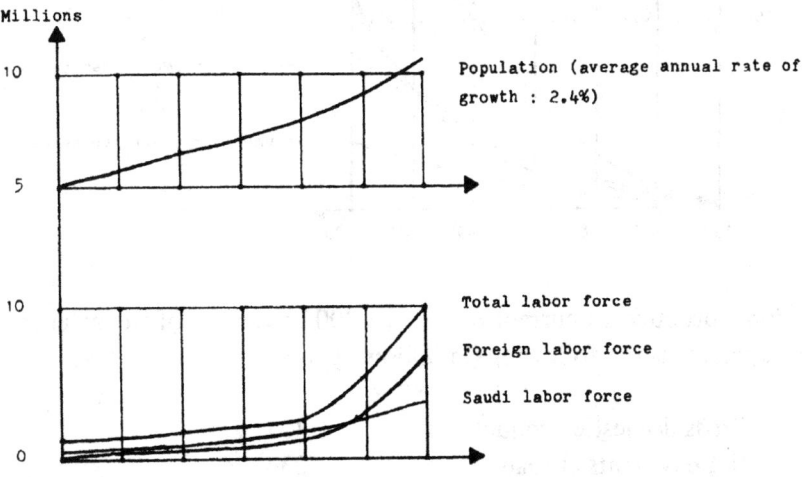

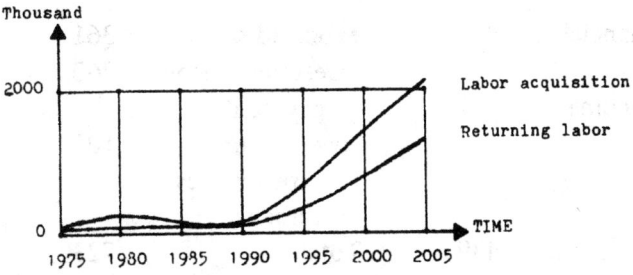

Figure 9.20: Payments Abroad

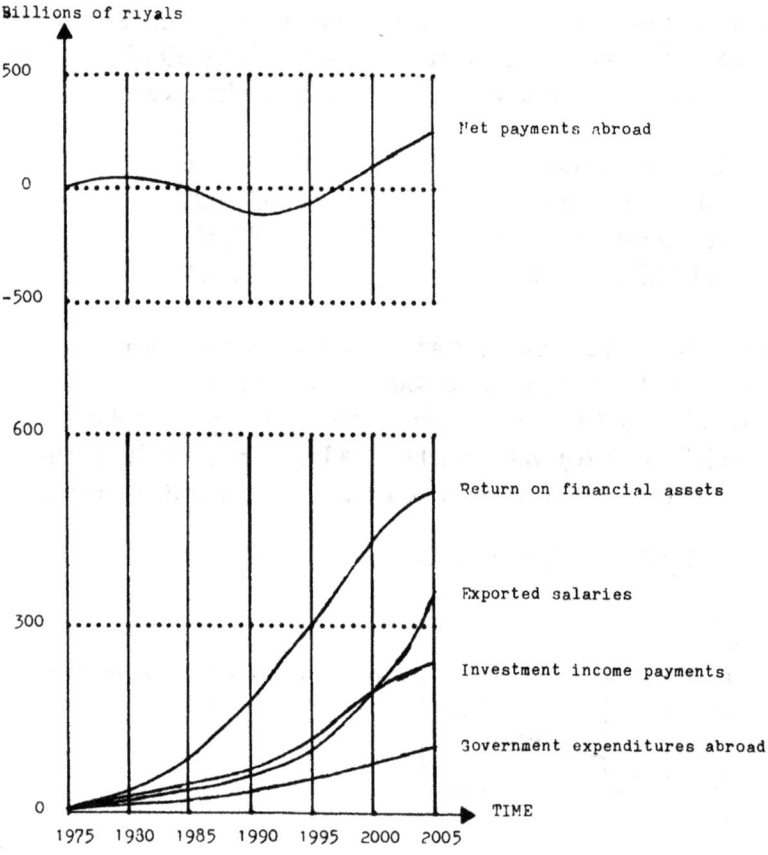

national product. In current prices, the 2005 situation of the balance of payments is the following (in billion riyals):

Gross domestic product	:	1,807
Net payments abroad	:	234
Gross national product	:	1,573

return on financial assets	487	exported salaries	361
pilgrimage income	2	investment income payments	260
		government expenditures abroad	102
Total:	489	Total:	723

The Management of the Economic Development   147

On the positive side, the result of a larger programme of government expenditures is a substantial accumulation of non-oil wealth (Figure 9.21) which reaches 6,271 billion riyals in 2005. However, the present results are not as good as the results of the simulation experiment of the fourth paragraph.

2005 Balance Sheet of the Economy (billion riyals)

Reserves of crude oil	:	19,962
Productive capital	:	1,853
Consumer durables	:	658
Financial assets	:	2,892
Inventory	:	277
2005 GNP	:	591
TOTAL	:	26,233
Population (millions)	:	10.17
Wealth per capita (riyals)	:	2,579,450

Figure 9.21: Wealth per capita

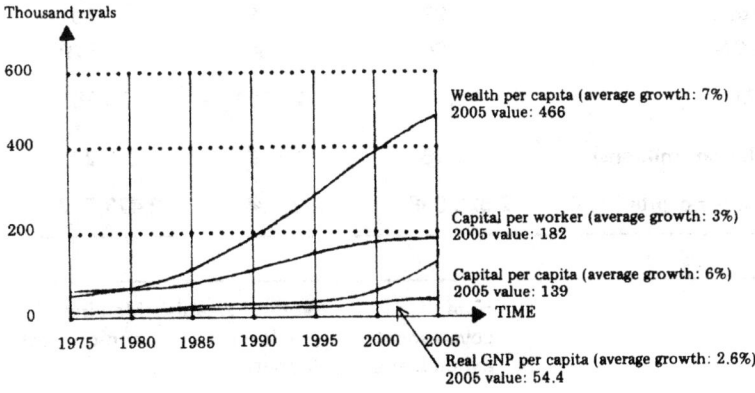

This means that it rapidly becomes very expensive to recycle more revenues domestically. These additional expenditures are all on account of foreign labour. Table 9.3 clearly indicates that a lack of domestic labour places severe restrictions upon the rate of economic growth. A rate of domestic development that is too high implies

148 The Strategies of Economic Development

Table 9.3: Domestic Development and Foreign Labour Force

	Inflation rate	Rate of government expenditures	2005 non-oil wealth (billion SR)	2005 foreign labour level
Experiment A	3.2%	12%	4,340	2,428,000
Fourth paragraph	3.1%	12%	6,510	3,583,000
Present	3.1%	14%	6,635	4,727,000
Present	3.2%	16%	6,270	6,290,000
Present	3.4%	18%	5,879	8,356,000
Present	3.6%	20%	5,511	11,354,000

Rate of government expenditures	14%	18%	20%
(in billion SR)			
Reserves of crude oil	20,036	19,892	19,771
Productive capital	1,517	2,320	3,014
Consumer durables	628	716	786
Financial assets	3,649	1,898	625
Inventory	236	361	507
2005 GNP	605	584	579
TOTAL	26,671	25,771	25,282
Population (millions)	10.16	10.19	10.22
Wealth per capita (riyals)	2,625,098	2,529,048	2,473,777

	Rate of government expenditures	Non-oil wealth per foreign labourer (thousand SR)	Marginal non-oil wealth (billion SR)
Experiment A	12%	1,787.5	—
Fourth paragraph	12%	1,816.9	2,170
Present	14%	1,403.6	125
Present	16%	996.8	−365
Present	18%	703.6	−391
Present	20%	485.4	−368

Figure 9.22: Surplus and Financial Assets with 14 per cent Average Annual Increase in Autonomous Investment

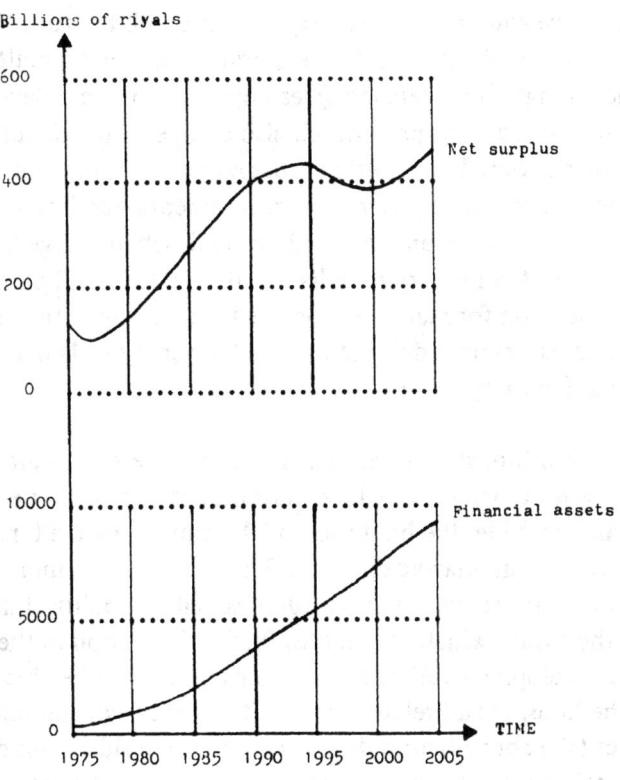

labour costs greater than labour returns resulting in a negative marginal accumulation of non-oil wealth. Thus, the present experiments suggest an optimal long-term growth in government expenditures of about fourteen per cent per year. This rate can be directly risen through an increase in the volume of domestic labour force, through increases in productivity or through the systematic selection of highly capital-intensive activities. However, an increase in either the quantity or the quality of the domestic labour generates increases in the national product, more demand and more labour demand. Similarly, capital-intensive activities call for labour-intensive industries.

The petrochemical and related projects are only the tip of the iceberg in spite of their immense size. Such development immediately generates demands for more and improved highways, ports, electric power, water, air transport, education, and housing. This kind of massive construction creates ever increasing economic expansion. The worker who builds housing must himself have a house in which to live and, in addition, requires automobiles, furniture, towels, carpets, shoes, soft drinks, potato chips, and a multitude of other things. Such demand gives impetus to further development of business enterprise which also competes for already scarce manpower. The resulting urbanization in turn creates the needs for more infrastructure and governmental services and so the process goes on seemingly without end. When a large increase in the size of the military establishment is added to all of this, the competition for manpower begins to reach the critical point. (H.H. Albers, seminar delivered at the University of Petroleum and Minerals, February 1976.)

Therefore, even though large amounts of capital resources are available, even though very high rates of domestic growth are theoretically possible, the limitation of the Saudi Arabian long-term rate of growth is an unavoidable fact. Besides, a massive importation of foreign labour has important cultural, social and political implications for the future which can lead to further limitation in the rate of economic development. Also, the economy might not be able to provide the housing and related services to such a high amount of expatriates (the above figures do not take into consideration dependants of workers). As a result, the accumulation of financial assets is a highly probable feature of the future of the Saudi Arabian economic development. A fourteen per cent average annual rate of government expenditures for example, leaves a very substantial part of the national wealth unemployed internally (Figure 9.22). The management of these assets is naturally very important because it is directly responsible for the equilibrium of the balance of payments. Saudi Arabia has chosen industrialization but will also have to practice banking on a very large scale. The success of this management will directly affect the success of the kingdom's domestic development.

The economic future of Saudi Arabia is bright but the task of the national leaders is arduous. They must constantly watch the inflation rate which, if too high, can severely damage the economy. They must seize every opportunity to develop the human resources of the kingdom. They must play an increasing role in international economics to protect the real value of their financial resources and last, but not least, they are in charge of the most valuable energy source of the twentieth century: oil.

10 CONCLUSION

The purpose of this book has been, through the outlining of a method that will serve as a working tool, to analyze the structure of the Saudi Arabian economy and to evaluate globally major development problems as well as possible achievements of the economy. This study, however, does not go beyond the stage of an introduction to a much larger field of analysis. The present work suggests three main directions for further research.

The most immediate development of this research consists of multiplying the number of experiments with the model. Several important points should be studied in more detail in order to identify more behaviour types of the model. This book has naturally presented the most important long-term results of changes in the key assumptions of the model such as inflation, government expenditures or crude oil production, but other structural or behavioural assumptions as well as policies have not been analyzed. In addition, the effect of potential policies that do not exist at present but could be implemented as a result of long-term changes in both the structure of the economy and the behaviour of the agents, should be considered.

A second task should be to improve the structure of the model as well as the experimentation procedure. The utilization of a more flexible simulation tool, now available, allows policy variables to be formulated before a simulation run and modified during the simulation process. As a result, this process is no more a totally mechanical procedure in which the analyst has a passive role but involves human decisions and subjective elements. Also, the improvement of the structure of the model would allow the introduction of more sectors and the analysis of more specific problems related to the input-output structure of the economy.

Finally, the model should be used as a general background to conduct more specific studies. The number of economic analyses dealing with the Saudi Arabian economy is still very small. The economic development presently taking place in the kingdom and the problems ahead will rapidly make such studies indispensable and call for a substantial development of the profession of economist in Saudi Arabia.

BIBLIOGRAPHY

This short bibliography lists the books, reviews and magazines or newspapers that have been utilized as a source of information of data. These publications are concerned with the methodology of system dynamics, development economics, the economy of Saudi Arabia and the economics of crude oil and energy. Most of the few publications concerned with the economy of Saudi Arabia are descriptive. To the author's knowledge, there are only two books that constitute an attempt to view the subject matter from an analytical perspective: Dr Faisal Bashir's *Econometric Model of the Saudi Arabian Economy*, and the present book.

Arabian American Oil Company, *Annual Reports 1974* and *1975*.
Arabian American Oil Company, *Facts and Figures, 1973, 1974, 1975.*
Bashir, F.S., *An Econometric Model of the Saudi Arabian Economy: 1960–1970*, Ph.D. dissertation, University of Arizona, 1973.
Blitzer, C., Meeraus, A., and Stoutjesdijk, A., 'A Dynamic Model of OPEC Trade and Production', *Journal of Development Economics*, Vol. 2, No. 4, December 1975.
Centre for Middle Eastern and Islamic Studies, University of Durham, *The Middle East Yearbook 1977*, Middle East Magazine Ltd, 1976.
Chatelus, M., *Strategies pour le Moyen Orient*, Calmann-Levy, Paris, 1974.
Fischer, D., Gately, D., and Kyle, J.F., 'The Prospects for OPEC, A Critical Survey of Models of the World Oil Market', *Journal of Development Economics*, Vol. 2, No. 4, December 1975.
Forrester, J.W., *Industrial Dynamics*, MIT Press, Cambridge, Mass., 1961.
Forrester, J.W., *Principles of Systems*, Wright Allen Press, Cambridge, Mass., 1968.
Industrial Studies and Development Centre, *Guide for Industrial Investment in Saudi Arabia*, Riyadh, 1972.
International Monetary Fund, *International Financial Statistics*, Vol. XXIX, No. 9, Washington D.C., September 1976.
Kalymon, B.A., 'Economic Incentives in OPEC Oil Pricing Policy', *Journal of Development Economics*, Vol. 2, No. 4, December 1975.
Kingdom of Saudi Arabia, Ministry of Planning, *The Second*

Development Plan 1975–1980, Riyadh, 1976.

Knauerhase, P., *The Saudi Arabian Economy*, Praeger, 1975.

Mallakh, P., and McGuire, C. (eds.), *Energy and Development, Proceedings of the International Conference on the Economics of Energy and Development*, International Research Center for Energy and Economic Development, Boulder, Colorado, 1974.

Masseron, J., *L'Economie des hydrocarbures*, Technip, 1969.

Morgan, T., *Economic Development: Concept and Strategy*, Harper and Row, New York, 1975.

Nelson, J.W., Short, R. and Mallakh, R., *The Arab Middle East: Economic Potential*, Stanford Research Institute, 1976.

Pugh III, A.L., *DYNAMO II User's Manual*, MIT Press, Cambridge, Mass., 1973.

Saudi Arabian Monetary Agency, *Annual Reports 1970, 1971, 1972, 1973, 1974, 1975*.

United Nations, *Studies on Selected Development Problems in Various Countries in the Middle East*, New York, 1969 and 1970.

United Nations, *Industrial Development in the Arab Countries*, New York, 1967.

Magazines and Newspapers (various issues)

Arab News
Business Week
Financial Times
Middle East Business Digest
Middle East Economic Digest
Le Monde
Newsweek
Petroleum Economist
Saudi Business
Saudi Gazette

APPENDIX I

```
MODEL MEMSA     3/14/77

* MODEL MEMSA
NOTE
NOTE RESERVES CF CRUDE OIL
NOTE
L  ORES.K=ORES.J+(DT)(DISCO.JK-COP.JK)
N  ORES=ORESI
C  ORESI=111200
R  DISCO.KL=(DIRAT.K)(ORES.K)
A  DIRAT.K=TABHL(DITAB,ACOP.K,25000,150000,25000)
T  DITAB=.06/.032/.018/.009/.003/0
L  ACOP.K=ACOP.J+(DT)(COP.JK)
N  ACOP=ACOPI
C  ACOPI=25677
NOTE
NOTE CRUDE OIL PRODUCTION
NOTE
R  COP.KL=COPEX.K+DOMUS.K
NOTE
NOTE PRODUCTION FOR EXPORT
NOTE
A  COPEX.K=PRN.K*ACMUL.K*OPMUL.K
N  COPEX=COPEXI
C  COPEXI=3260
A  PRN.K=(TABHL(OILTAB,SRPR.K,0,50,10))(365)
T  OILTAB=0/5/8/9/9/9
A  SRPR.K=SMOOTH(ORES.K/COP.JK,DSR)
C  DSR=3
A  ACMUL.K=TABHL(TACMUL,SAOR.K,1,5,1)
T  TACMUL=1/1/1/1/1
A  SAOR.K=SMOOTH(FINAS.K/GNP.K,DSRA)
C  DSRA=3
A  OPMUL.K=TABHL(TOPMUL,SP.K,10,30,5)
T  TOPMUL=1/1/1/1/1
NOTE
NOTE DOMESTIC USAGE
NOTE
A  DOMUS.K=EOR.K*VNUP.JK
A  EOR.K=TABHL(TEOR,CAPWO.K,50,150,25)
T  TEOR=.00167/.00167/.00167/.00167/.00167
A  CAPWO.K=SMOOTH(CAP.K/TLF.K,DSRR)
C  DSRR=5
NOTE
NOTE GROSS DOMESTIC OIL PRODUCT
NOTE
A  GDPOIL.K=SP.K*ERSR*COPEX.K
C  ERSR=3.5
NOTE
NOTE PRICE OF CRUDE OIL
NOTE
A  SP.K=SMOOTH(PRICE.K,DSP)
N  SP=SPI
C  SPI=12.4
C  DSP=2
A  PRICE.K=SUP.K-(COPEX.K/(DWDA.K*EXP(TIM.K*LOGN(1+RGWD.K))))
A  SUP.K=SUPI*EXP(TIM.K*LOGN(1+RGSUP))
C  SUPI=30
C  RGSUP=0
A  DWDA.K=3200/(SUP.K-12.4)
```

```
MODEL MEMSA    3/14/77

A  RGWD.K=TABHL(TRGWD,SP.K,10,30,5)
T  TRGWD=.052/.049/.043/.031/0
NOTE
NOTE SUPPLY TO CONSUMERS
NOTE
L  UFOC.K=UFOC.J+(DT)(VCDEM.JK-SSC.JK)
N  UFOC=UFOCI
C  UFOCI=52650
R  SSC.KL=UFCC.K/DFOC.K
A  DFOC.K=TABHL(TCFOC,STOCK.K/SCDEM.K,.5,2,.25)
T  TDFOC=5.5/3.2/2/1.25/1/.8/.6
NOTE
NOTE SUPPLY TO AUTONOMCUS INVESTMENT
NOTE
L  UFOAI.K=UFOAI.J+(DT)(VAINV.JK-SSAI.JK)
N  UFOAI=UFOAII
C  UFOAII=20350
R  SSAI.KL=UFOAI.K/DFOAI.K
A  DFOAI.K=TABHL(TDFOI,STOCK.K/SAIDEM.K,.5,2,.25)
T  TDFOI=8/5.15/3.75/3/2.8/2.75/2.75
NOTE
NOTE SUPPLY TC INDUCED INVESTMENT
NOTE
L  UFOII.K=UFOII.J+(DT)(IINV.JK-SSII.JK)
N  UFOII=UFOIII
C  UFOIII=20350
R  SSII.KL=UFOII.K/DFOII.K
A  DFOII.K=TABHL(TDFOI,STOCK.K/SIIDEM.K,.5,2,.25)
NOTE
NOTE INVENTORY
NOTE
L  STOCK.K=STOCK.J+(DT)(VNOP.JK+IMPORT.JK-SSC.JK-SSAI.JK-SSII.JK)
N  STOCK=STOCKI
C  STOCKI=22230
NOTE
NOTE NCN OIL PRODUCTION
NOTE
R  VNOP.KL=MIN(PCAP.K,PCLAB.K)
N  VNOP=VNOPI
C  VNOPI=27485
A  PCAP.K=CAP.K/COR.K
A  PCLAB.K=PCSL.K+PCFL.K
A  PCSL.K=(SLF.K*NHW)/SLOR.K
A  PCFL.K=(FLF.K*NHW)/FLOR.K
C  NHW=1.76
NOTE
NOTE IMPORT
NOTE
R  IMPORT.KL=DELAY1(DESIMP.K,IDEL)
C  IDEL=.25
A  DESIMP.K=(DVNOP.K-VNCP.JK)/AD
C  AD=1
NOTE
NOTE DESIRED NCN OIL PRODUCTION
NOTE
A  DVNOP.K=STDEM.K+((DSTOCK.K-STOCK.K)/ADD)
N  DVNOP=DVNCPI
C  DVNOPI=50000
```

Appendix I

```
MODEL MEMSA    3/14/77

C ADD=2
NOTE
NOTE DESIRED INVENTORY
NOTE
A DSTOCK.K=STM.K*STSS.K
A STM.K=TABHL(TSTM,SSG.K,0,.2,.02)
T TSTM=.6/.6/.6/.6/.6/.6/.6/.6/.6/.6/.6
A SSG.K=SMOOTH(SG.K,DSSG)
C DSSG=2
A  SG.K=(TTSS.JK-TSSPP.JK)/(TSSPP.JK*DT)
N SG=SGI
C SGI=.2
R TTSS.KL=TSS.K
R TSSPP.KL=TTSS.JK
A TSS.K=SSC.JK+SSAI.JK+SSII.JK
A STSS.K=SMOOTH(TSS.K,DSTS)
C DSTS=2
NOTE
NOTE POPULATION
NOTE
L POP.K=POP.J+(DT)(NB.JK-ND.JK)
N POP=POPI
C POPI=4946
R NB.KL=BR.K*POP.K
A BR.K=TABHL(BRTAB,SRGNPC.K,20,50,5)
T BRTAB=.048/.044/.04/.0375/.035/.034/.032
A SRGNPC.K=SMOOTH((GNP.K/PRIND.K)/POP.K,DSGNP)
C DSGNP=5
R ND.KL=DR.K*POP.K
A DR.K=TABHL(CRTAB,SWPC.K,40,360,80)
T DRTAB=.02/.0148/.012/.0104/.01
A SWPC.K=SMOOTH(TCAP.K/POP.K,DSWPC)
C DSWPC=5
A TCAP.K=CAP.K+CCAP.K+(FINAS.K/PRIND.K)
NOTE
NOTE SAUDI LABOR FORCE
NOTE
A SLF.K=AM.K*POP.K
A AM.K=TABHL(TAM,TIME.K,1975,2015,5)
T TAM=.26/.265/.27/.28/.3/.32/.35/.39/.45
A SLOR.K=TABHL(SLORTAB,SCAPCA.K,20,55,5)
T SLORTAB=.138/.138/.091/.069/.054/.047/.044/.041
A SCAPCA.K=SMOOTH(CAP.K/POP.K,DSCPC)
C DSCPC=5
NOTE
NOTE FOREIGN LABOR FORCE
NOTE
L FLF.K=FLF.J+(DT)(NLA.JK-RLAB.JK)
N FLF=FLFI
C FLFI=314
R NLA.KL=DELAY3(FLDE.K,LCD)
C LCD=.5
A FLDE.K=(PCAP.K-PCLAB.K)(FLOR.K)/NHW
A FLOR.K=TABHL(TFLOR,CAPWO.K,50,150,25)
T TFLOR=.05/.05/.045/.042/.04
R RLAB.KL=FLF.K/ADFC
C ADFC=4
A TLF.K=SLF.K+FLF.K
```

158 *Appendix I*

```
MODEL MEMSA    3/14/77
NOTE
NOTE PRODUCTIVE CAPITAL
NOTE
L  CAP.K=CAP.J+(DT)(ACAC.JK+ICAC.JK-CDEP.JK)
N  CAP=CAPI
C  CAPI=115437
R  ACAC.KL=DELAY1(SSAI.JK,ACAD)
C  ACAD=.3
A  AINV.K=TABHL(TAINV,TIME.K,1975,2015,5)
T  TAINV=10000/17700/31400/55600/98500/174500/309100/547600/970200
R  VAINV.KL=AINV.K/PRIND.K
R  ICAC.KL=DELAY1(SSII.JK,ICAD)
C  ICAD=.3
R  IINV.KL=MAX((DESCAP.K-CAP.K)/ADE,0)
C  ADE=4
A  TCAC.K=ACAC.JK+ICAC.JK
A  VIDE.K=VAINV.JK+IINV.JK
R  CDEP.KL=CAP.K*ROD
C  ROD=.05
A  DESCAP.K=DVNOP.K*COR.K
A  COR.K=TABHL(CORTAB,SRGNPC.K,20,50,5)
T  CORTAB=3.5/3.5/3.5/3.5/3.5/3.5/3.5
N  COR=CORI
C  CORI=3.5
NOTE
NOTE FINANCIAL ASSETS
NOTE
L  FINAS.K=FINAS.J+(DT)(NSUR.JK)
N  FINAS=FINASI
C  FINASI=138645
R  NSUR.KL=GNP.K-(SSC.JK+ACAC.JK+ICAC.JK)(PRIND.K)
NOTE
NOTE INFLATION
NOTE
L  PRIND.K=PRIND.J+(DT)(NPVAR.JK)
N  PRIND=PRINDI
C  PRINDI=1
R  NPVAR.KL=PRRG.K*PRIND.K
A  PRRG.K=SMOOTH(SEF.K+IPEF.K+DEF.K,DSPV)
C  DSPV=2
N  PRRG=PRRGI
C  PRRGI=0
A  SEF.K=((SAL.K-EXSAL.K)/GNP.K)(RGSA.K-RGOM.K)
A  IPEF.K=(IMPORT.JK/(GNP.K/PRIND.K))*RGIP.K
A  RGIP.K=TABHL(TRGIP,TIME.K,1975,2015,5)
T  TRGIP=.15/.06/.035/.023/.02/.02/.02/.02
A  DEF.K=TABHL(DEFTA,STSDR.K,.3,1,.1)
T  DEFTA=.1/.045/.025/.012/.007/0/0/0
A  STSDR.K=SMOOTH(TSS.K/TDEM.K,DSRAT)
C  DSRAT=2
NOTE
NOTE GROSS DOMESTIC PRODUCT
NOTE
A  GDP.K=GDPOIL.K+GDPNOIL.K
A  GDPNOIL.K=VNOP.JK*PRIND.K
NOTE
NOTE GROSS NATIONAL PRODUCT
NOTE
```

Appendix I

```
MODEL MEMSA    3/14/77

A  GNP.K=GDP.K-NPAB.K
N  GNP=GNPI
C  GNPI=1200C0
NOTE
NOTE CONSUMER DEMAND
NOTE
R  VCDEM.KL=CDEM.K/PRIND.K
A  SCDEM.K=SMOOTH(VCDEM.JK,DSCD)
C  DSCD=2
A  CDEM.K=(MPC.K)(GOVMUL.K)(DELAY1(GNP.K,DIC))
C  DIC=.4
A  MPC.K=MPCN*INMUL.K*PAMU.K*WMUL.K
N  MPC=MPCI
C  MPCI=.65
C  MPCN=.75
A  INMUL.K=TABHL(TINMUL,PRRG.K,.05,.45,.05)
T  TINMUL=1/1/1/1/1/1/1/1/1
A  PAMU.K=TABHL(PATA,SSDR.K,.3,1,.1)
T  PATA=.3/.33/.37/.41/.5/.6/.78/1
A  SSDR.K=SMOOTH(SSC.JK/VCDEM.JK,DSRT)
C  DSRT=2
A  WMUL.K=TABHL(WMUTA,SWPC.K,40,360,80)
T  WMUTA=1/1/.96/.85/.8
A  GOVMUL.K=TABHL(GOTAB,TIME.K,1975,2015,5)
T  GOTAB=1/1/1/1/1/1/1/1/1
NOTE
NOTE CONSUMERS DURABLES
NOTE
L  CCAP.K=CCAP.J+(DT)(CDAC.JK-CDDEP.JK)
N  CCAP=CCAPI
C  CCAPI=25000
R  CDAC.KL=PCD*SSC.JK
C  PCD=.3
R  CDDEP.KL=CCAP.K/ADCD
C  ADCD=15
NOTE
NOTE INVESTMENT DEMAND
NOTE
A  IDEM.K=AINV.K+(IINV.JK*PRIND.K)
A  SAIDEM.K=SMOOTH(VAINV.JK,DSAID)
C  DSAID=2
A  SIIDEM.K=SMOOTH(IINV.JK,DSIID)
C  DSIID=2
NOTE
NOTE TOTAL DEMAND
NOTE
A  TDEM.K=VCDEM.JK+VAINV.JK+IINV.JK
A  STDEM.K=SMOOTH(TDEM.K,DSDE)
C  DSDE=2
NOTE
NOTE SALARIES AND WAGES
NOTE
A  SAL.K=AAS.K*TLF.K
L  AAS.K=AAS.J+(DT)(NSVAR.JK)
N  AAS=AASI
C  AASI=17.179
R  NSVAR.KL=(RGSL.K)(AAS.K)
A  RGSL.K=MAX(RGSA.K,0)
```

Appendix I

```
MODEL MEMSA      3/14/77

A RGSA.K=SMOOTH(PRRG.K+RGOM.K,DSGSA)
C DSGSA=3
N RGSA=RGSAI
C RGSAI=.2
A RGOM.K=(OM.JK-POM.JK)/(POM.JK*DT)
N RGOM=RGOMI
C RGOMI=.012
R POM.KL=OM.JK
R OM.KL=VNOP.JK/TLF.K
NOTE
NOTE PROFITS
NOTE
A PROF.K=GNP.K-(SAL.K-EXSAL.K)
NOTE
NOTE PAYMENTS ABROAD
NOTE
A NPAB.K=EXSAL.K+IIP.K+GEA.K-PIL.K-ROFA.K
NOTE
NOTE EXPORTED SALARIES
NOTE
A EXSAL.K=EPS.K*AAS.K*FLF.K
A EPS.K=EPSN*PAMUL.K*INMU.K
C EPSN=.6
A PAMUL.K=TABHL(PAMUTA,SSDR.K,.3,1,.1)
T PAMUTA=1/1/.99/.98/.96/.92/.87/.8
A INMU.K=TABHL(INMUTA,PRRG.K,.05,.45,.05)
T INMUTA=1/1.01/1.02/1.04/1.05/1.08/1.09/1.1/1.1
NOTE
NOTE INVESTMENT INCOME PAYMENTS
NOTE
A IIP.K=DELAY1(PFP.K*PROF.K,DEP)
C DEP=.75
A PFP.K=TABHL(PFPTAB,SLF.K/TLF.K,.1,1,.1)
T PFPTAB=.4/.39/.36/.32/.25/.18/.1/.05/.05/.05
NOTE
NOTE GOVERNMENT EXPENDITURES ABROAD
NOTE
A GEA.K=PGH.K*GDP.K
A PGH.K=TABHL(PGHTAB,TIME.K,1975,2015,5)
T PGHTAB=.07/.07/.07/.068/.065/.061/.058/.051/.045
NOTE
NOTE PILGRIMAGE
NOTE
A PIL.K=PILI*EXP(TIM.K*LOGN(1+RGPIL.K))
C PILI=1665
A RGPIL.K=TABHL(TRGPIL,TIME.K,1975,2015,5)
T TRGPIL=.1/.066/.042/.027/.015/.007/0/0/0
NOTE
NOTE RETURN ON FINANCIAL ASSETS
NOTE
A ROFA.K=DELAY1(ROR.K*FINAS.K,RFAD)
C RFAD=1
A ROR.K=TABHL(RORTAB,TIME.K,1975,2015,5)
T RORTAB=.065/.065/.065/.065/.065/.065/.065/.065/.065
NOTE
NOTE
NOTE
N TIME=NTIME
```

Appendix I

```
MODEL MEMSA    3/14/77
  C NTIME=1976
  A TIM.K=TIME.K-NTIME
  C DT=.1
  C LENGTH=2015
  C PRTPER=1
  C PLTPER=1
NOTE
NOTE
NOTE
PRINT ORES/*/NPAB/*/FLDE/VCDEM,CDEM/*/GDPOIL/UFOC/SSC/DFOC/SAL/AAS
PRINT DISCO/*/GNP/PRRG/NLA/VAINV,AINV/*/GCPNOIL/UFOAI/SSAI/DFOAI/PRO
PRINT RGSA
PRINT */COP/*/PRIND/RLAB/IINV,IDEM/*/GDP/LFGII/SSII/DFOII/RGSL/*
PRINT ACOP/COPEX/EXSAL/*/*/VIDE/*/*/*/*/*/*/SSG
PRINT */PRN/IIP/POP/CAP/*/TDEM/*/IMPORT/SSDR/TSS/ACAC/DEF/*
PRINT SRPR/*/GEA/SLF/DESCAP/STOCK/*/*/DESIMP/STSDR/*/ICAC/IFEF/CM
PRINT */*/*/FLF/*/DSTOCK/PCAP/*/*/*/*/*/SEF,RGOM
PRINT DIRAT/DOMUS/ROFA/TLF/FINAS/*/PCSL/*/TCAP/SRGNPC,SWPC/TCAC/*/*
PRINT */*/PIL/*/*/VNOP/PCFL/*/*/SCAPCA/SAOR/*/BR,DR
PRINT RGWD/SP/*/MPC/NSUR/DVNOP,PCLAB/*/*/CAPWO/*/*/SLOR,FLOR
PRINT SUP/CCAP
NOTE
NOTE
NOTE
PLOT COP,DISCO
PLOT ACOP,ORES
PLOT SRPR
PLOT SP,SUP
PLOT GDPOIL
PLOT POP
PLOT TLF,SLF,FLF
PLOT FLDE,NLA,RLAB
PLOT DESCAP,CAP
PLOT VIDE,TCAC
PLOT DVNOP,VNOP,PCAP,PCLAB,IMPORT
PLOT STOCK,DSTOCK
PLOT SSDR,STSOR
PLOT TDEM,TSS
PLOT NSUR
PLOT FINAS
PLOT SAOR
PLOT TCAP
PLOT PRRG
PLOT PRIND
PLOT GDP,GDPOIL,GDPNOIL
PLOT GNP,CDEM,VCDEM,SSC
PLOT SAL,PROF
PLOT AAS,OM
PLOT NPAB
PLOT ROFA,GEA,EXSAL,IIP
PLOT CAPWO,SCAPCA,SRGNPC,SWPC
RUN
```

APPENDIX II

AAS	Average annual salary (thousand SR)
AASI	Initial average annual salary (thousand SR/year)
ACAC	Autonomous capital acquisition (million SR/year)
ACMUL	Absorption multiplier (dimensionless)
ACOP	Cumulative crude oil production (million bbl)
AD	Adjustment delay for desired import (years)
ADCD	Average duration of consumer durables (years)
ADD	Adjustment delay for desired volume of non-oil production (years)
ADE	Adjustment delay for induced investment (years)
ADFC	Average duration of foreigners' labour contracts (years)
AINV	Autonomous investment (million SR/year)
AM	Activity multiplier (% year)
BR	Birth rate (% year)
CAP	Total productive capital (million SR)
CAPWO	Smoothed productive capital per worker (thousand SR)
CCAP	Stock of consumer durables (million SR)
CDAC	Acquisition of consumer durables (million SR/year)
CDDEP	Depreciation of consumer durables (million SR/year)
CDEM	Consumer demand (million SR/year)
CDEP	Productive capital depreciation (million SR/year)
COP	Total crude oil production (million bbl/year)
COPEX	Crude oil production for export (million bbl/year)
COR	Capital output ratio (dimensionless)
DEF	Demand effect on inflation (% year)
DESCAP	Desired capital (million SR/year)
DESIMP	Desired import (million SR/year)
DFOAI	Delay filling orders from autonomous investment (years)
DFOC	Delay filling orders from consumer demand (years)
DFOII	Delay filling orders from induced investment (year)
DIRAT	Rate of crude oil discovery (% year)
DISCO	Crude oil discoveries (million bbl/year)
DOMUS	Domestic usage of crude oil (million bbl/year)
DR	Death rate (% year)
DSTOCK	Desired inventory (million SR/year)
DT	Computation time period

Appendix II

DVNOP	Desired volume of non-oil production (million SR/year)
DWDA	Decrease in world demand for oil per additional US $ in price (million bbl/year)
EOR	Energy output ratio (bbl/SR)
EPS	Exported proportion of expatriates' salaries (% year)
EPSN	Normal exported proportion of expatriates' salaries (% year)
ERSR	Rate of exchange of the Saudi riyal (SR per US $)
EXSAL	Exported salaries (million SR/year)
FINAS	Financial assets (million SR)
FLDE	Foreign labour demand (thousand/year)
FLF	Foreign labour force (thousand)
FLOR	Foreign labour output ratio (hours worked per SR of value added)
GDP	Gross domestic product (million SR/year)
GDPNOIL	Gross domestic product, non-oil sector (million SR/year)
GDPOIL	Gross domestic product, oil sector (million SR/year)
GEA	Government expenditures abroad (million SR/year)
GNP	Gross national product (million SR/year)
GOVMUL	Government multiplier for consumption demand (dimensionless)
ICAC	Induced capital acquisition (million SR/year)
IDEM	Investment demand (million SR/year)
IINV	Induced investment demand (million SR/year)
IIP	Investment income payments (million SR/year)
IMPORT	Imports (million SR/year)
INMU	Inflation multiplier (dimensionless)
INMUL	Inflation multiplier (dimensionless)
IPEF	Import effect on inflation (% year)
MPC	Propensity to consume (% year)
MPCN	Normal propensity to consume (% year)
MWD	Maximum world oil demand to Saudi Arabia (million bbl)
NB	Number of births (thousand/year)
ND	Number of deaths (thousand/year)
NHW	Number of man hours per year (thousand/year)
NLA	Net labour acquisition (thousand/year)
NPAB	Net payments abroad (million SR/year)
NPVAR	Net price variation (dimensionless)
NSUR	Net surplus (million SR/year)

Appendix II

NSVAR	Salary variation (thousand SR/year)
OM	Output per man (thousand SR/year)
OPMUL	Price multiplier (dimensionless)
ORES	Reserves of crude oil (million bbl)
PAMU	Product availability multiplier (dimensionless)
PAMUL	Product availability multiplier (dimensionless)
PCAP	Production capacity from capital (million SR/year)
PCD	Proportion of consumer durables in total consumption (% year)
PCFL	Production capacity from foreign labour force (million SR/year)
PCLAB	Production capacity from total labour force (million SR/year)
PCSL	Production capacity from Saudi labour force (million SR/year)
PFP	Proportion of repatriated profits (% year)
PGH	Proportion of government help (% year)
PIL	Income from pilgrimages (million SR/year)
PILI	Initial income from pilgrimages (million SR/year)
POM	Output per man; previous period (thousand SR/year)
POP	Saudi population (thousand)
PRICE	Price of crude oil (US $/bbl)
PRIND	Price index (dimensionless)
PRN	Normal extraction rate (million bbl/day)
PROF	Total profits after payments abroad (million SR/year)
PRRG	Price rate of growth (% year)
RGIP	Rate of growth of import prices (% year)
RGOM	Rate of growth of the output per man (% year)
RGPIL	Rate of growth of pilgrimage revenues (% year)
RGSA	Rate of growth of the average annual salary (% year)
RGSL	Rate of growth of the average annual salary (% year)
RGSUP	Rate of growth of the substitution price (% year)
RGWD	Rate of growth of the world oil demand (% year)
RLAB	Returning labour force (thousand/year)
ROD	Rate of depreciation of productive capital (% year)
ROFA	Return on financial assets (million SR/year)
ROR	Rate of return on financial assets (% year)
SAIDEM	Smoothed autonomous investment demand (million SR/year)
SAL	Salaries and wages (million SR/year)
SAOR	Smoothed financial asset to GNP ratio (years)

Appendix II

SCAPCA	Smoothed productive capital per capita (thousand SR/year)
SCDEM	Smoothed consumer demand (million SR/year)
SEF	Salary effect on inflation (% year)
SG	Shipment growth (% year)
SIIDEM	Smoothed induced investment demand (million SR/year)
SLF	Saudi labour force (thousand/year)
SLOR	Saudi labour output ratio (hours worked per riyal of value added)
SP	Smoothed price of crude oil (US $/bbl)
SRGNPC	Smoothed real GNP per capita (thousand SR/year)
SRPR	Smoothed reserve production ratio (years)
SSAI	Shipments sent to autonomous investment (million SR/year)
SSC	Shipments sent to consumers (million SR/year)
SSDR	Smoothed supply demand ratio for consumer goods (% year)
SSG	Smoothed shipment growth (% year)
SSII	Shipments sent to induced investment (million SR/year)
STDEM	Smoothed total demand (million SR/year)
STM	Inventory multiplier (years)
STOCK	Inventory (million SR)
STSDR	Smoothed total supply to total demand ratio (% year)
STSS	Smoothed shipments sent (million SR/year)
SUP	Substitution price (US $/bbl)
SUPI	Initial substitution price (US $/bbl)
SWPC	Smoothed wealth per capita (thousand SR/year)
t	Time (0, 1, 2, 3, etc.)
TCAC	Total volume of capital acquisition (million SR/year)
TCAP	Total capital (million SR)
TDEM	Total demand (million SR/year)
TIME	Time (Gregorian year)
TLF	Total labour force (thousand/year)
TSS	Total shipments sent (million SR/year)
UFOAI	Unfilled orders of autonomous investment (million SR)
UFOC	Unfilled orders of consumer goods (million SR)
UFOII	Unfilled orders of induced investment (million SR)
VAINV	Volume of autonomous investment demand (million SR/year)
VCDEM	Volume of consumer demand (million SR/year)

VIDE	Total volume of investment demand (million SR/year)
VNOP	Volume of non-oil production (million SR/year)
WMUL	Wealth multiplier (dimensionless)

INDEX

absorptive capacity 9, 42, 57, 93, 150
activity multiplier 50
auxiliary variable 16, 17

balance of payments 76 ff, 122, 123, 134, 146
balance sheet 125, 126, 133, 142, 147
birth rate 47, 49

capital adjustment 61, 62
capital depreciation 55, 61
capital output ratio 56, 57, 61, 62
consumer demand 40, 41, 71, 128

death rate 47, 49
delay functions 36, 40, 43, 44, 83, 91, 100
desired production 40, 113

energy output ratio 31, 32, 33
exogenous variables 90

factors of production 47
feed back loops 15-17, 25, 41, 58, 60-3, 67, 80-2, 91-6
financial assets 10, 45, 55, 57, 58, 63, 93, 115, 116, 149
flow 16, 17
foreign labour force 51, 61, 111, 147, 148

Government expenditures 53, 54, 143, 148
Government expenditures abroad 77, 78
Gross Domestic Product 21, 70, 119, 145
Gross National Product 70, 73, 120, 145

imports 40, 66, 114
industrialization 92, 106, 150
inflation 9, 42, 65 ff, 74, 93, 117, 118, 128
inventory 40, 42, 114
inventory multiplier 44

investment 53, 55, 143
investment income payments 77, 123, 146

labour efficiency 50, 52
labour force 52, 111, 136, 144, 145
level 16, 17, 96

model 9, 15, 16, 83, 107

national accounts 70 ff
national income 70
non-oil production 41, 42, 110, 113, 139
non-oil sector 15, 39 ff, 63, 106

oil discovery 23, 136
oil price 26-9, 109, 138, 139, 140
oil production 9, 19, 20, 22, 26, 108, 138-40
oil production policy 31, 32, 106, 137
oil reserves 19, 22, 25, 108, 139
oil revenues 20, 109
oil sector 15, 19, 25, 94, 105
oil (substitution price for) 27-9, 127
oil (world demand for) 33-5, 138
OPEC 10, 24, 26, 34

per capita indicators 124, 132, 141, 142
pilgrimage 78, 82
planning 10, 42
policy 88, 89, 92, 101
population 47, 59, 60, 111
price index 66, 67, 118
production capacity 51
production function 39
productive capital 47, 53, 62, 112
profit 74, 77, 94, 121
propensity to consume 71, 74-6

quantification procedure 97

reserve production ratio 24, 32, 136
return on financial assets 78, 123, 146

salary 71, 77, 121, 122
Saudi labour force 47, 50, 60, 111, 145
simulation experiments 88, 89, 95
smooth functions 36, 83
structural assumptions 88
structure 18, 91, 100
surplus 54, 57, 72, 93, 116, 141, 149
system dynamics 15, 95, 97, 136

table functions 29, 37, 43, 44, 49-51, 56, 68, 69, 75, 76, 79, 80, 88, 99, 129-31

wealth per capita 126, 132, 133, 142, 147